Undercover President

Grace Tee

ISBN-10:1517569028
ISBN-13:978-15169020

Published By
Mighty Pen Visions

Books support
Children's Lives Matter
(A children's education initiative)

DEDICATION

To the ruling Kingdom of this generation.
To the adults of this generation.
"Children's Lives Matter."

Contents

ACKNOWLEDGMENTS

To the children of the world, suffering from, emotional abuse, aids, landmines, sexual abuse, poverty, wars and lack of education.

To The Almighty, Omnipresent, Omniscient, We Seek Wisdom

"Children's Lives Really Matter"

Prologue

I feel a warm light inside me. It brightens my soul and makes me see life clearly. My conscience awakens as the light shines brightly. When the rain comes, it displays a rainbow, at the end of its showers. The rainbow reflects colours of the universe, none less colourful with no affiliation to race, colour or gender. The sun radiates a vibrant energy as it shines on the just and the unjust.. Nature awaits in its flora and fauna, to grace the earth, with no affiliation race to colour, or gender. It longs for anyone with time to spare and explore.

The vast oceans say to me....

"Come, I will guide you to the underworld, where sea life has its own kingdom."

It signals me without stereotyping. Nature in its grandiose calls me to come and find peace. The water flows in pristine style and says.

"Come human beings, stand still, and feel the wonders of my showers."

The animals remain sane in places where their natural world is reducing. They give a sold out show of how they cope when everything around them is changing. The mountains grace the soils of the earth with majesty and towering crowns.

The flowers emit perfumes which entice us to immerse the wonders of creation. We still believe that indeed it is a beautiful world.

Why does my heart sometimes gravitate towards darkness where no light endures? Is it human nature? Inclinations to hurt, hate, mistreat and being insensitive, all these vices I feel them in the dark part of my mind.

How can I keep sane in a world filled with diversity, hate, divisions and classes? How can I fulfil my God-given purpose in a world that has already defined who I am to be?

I am me, I am special. I have a purpose on this planet, and mine is to live.

I Have a Nightmare

Daniel struggled to wake up. Something was stifling him. A supernatural force as if it's holding him down. The force was pressing hard on his shoulders and pushing him into an abyss. A dark and dingy place, cold and unfriendly. He tried hard to muffle the crying and screaming noises. His fingers could not help, his hands failed him and his body was shaking from the wailing and shrieking small voices. It was the sound and presence of the children which kept him alert. They are crying and helpless in this dark and dangerous space. He can hear their small whining cries as he draws near. The kids are in pain, undernourished, sick, abused and bruised. Their eyes, the small and pleading eyes with dry tears on their cheeks. Children with severed limbs, disfigured they scamper.

Daniel cannot reach out to the kids something is holding him back. Emaciated with kwashiorkor and boogies on their little faces, they cry for help. He wants to reach out to the billion kids in this forgotten space. They know he can do something to relieve them from this, forever pain. The weight of the children's pain overwhelms Daniel.

"Help, help, please help us."

"Wake up Daniel, are you having nightmares again?" Maya shook her husband vigorously.

****

3

In the octagon office, Caleb was already stuck in his daily assignments. The President came to check on his diary.

"Are you out of your mind? Caleb, we are not in the movies. Running a country is not the same as reading from a script. Life is real, which President in his right mind can do such a crazy stunt. Have you gone totally bonkers?"

President Daniel Simba visibly angry, went and stood by the window looking into a distant space. Caleb Biti, his personal adviser, was checking his paperwork as his Instagram, Tweeter and email messages kept beeping on his computer and iPhone.

Caleb looked at President Daniel Simba with a smug on his face. He was clearly unaffected as if it's a social discussion about a tennis match which he always lost. He carried on surfing, on the web, glued on a popular culture news blog then looked at President Simba.

"Mr President, please hear me out, it is something to think about. Yes, you can secretly go undercover, visit real Kushians, your people. Go and see for yourself, the state of this nation and then address the people's problems. Be the first to rule from grass-roots than from bulletproof Kush House and sealed presidential cars."

"It's never too late to make a change for the benefit of the ordinary people. This is the era to create our own philosophy and social order."

4

"There is a first for everything Dan. Let's revolutionise politics by going to grass-roots level."

"Do not rely on political manifestos, media sentiments and Machiavellian philosophy." Caleb looked serious and unfazed by Daniel's stern and surprised look.

"No ways, Hozay, undercover; my foot! You of all my staff, you say such a load of hogwash? Have you been watching too many movies again; get real Caleb?"

Daniel protested while Caleb kept blogging and tweeting, glued to his laptop.

"Caleb do you understand the complexities of running a government. It's tricky enough these days, people stalk pastors in your beloved churches. They even record and hack information online and take note of every step, then tear you down, what more a country with 15 million people?"

"What about the international community? What about the election sponsors and interest groups? I am not safe as it is."

Daniel walked closer to Caleb as he carried on surfing and tapped him on his shoulder.

"Caleb, tell me something; why have I kept you for this long. I think you have lost your marbles.

I thought we are playing this political game of chase so well and still keeping our intellect. It is a complicated game to deal with daily."

"This is Kush country, not some imaginary Popeye cartoon land."

"Dan, Zip it!" Caleb abruptly stood up, raising his index finger,

"You know I was with you from the start of this game. Hello! Remember I was with you from Kush rural village. We went to Harvard and then came back into Kush House. Our current position is complex, I agree, and we might not be as savvy as we expected."

Caleb slammed his laptop and stood with arms akimbo.

"Listen to me Daniel; let's talk in simple terms; the rivers have not run dry in Kush land. We have enough timber and cement to build houses. We still have enough land to get people to plant food and feed families."

"Kushians have never asked for handouts it's not within them, their determination is to succeed despite the constipated existence. It is an economic system we are engineering for them, they are resilient, hard-working people. All they need is leadership and opportunities to develop their communities just like any progressive society."

Caleb is the personal adviser to President Daniel Simba the second black president-elect of Kush Republic. An educated and soft-spoken man.

Caleb's suggestion kept Simba frazzled and irritable. He dreaded his next meeting with the Minister of Defence. Since Simba's coming into office, he did not change the defence team. Mobo was a well known Army general and served in the late President Zorro's cabinet.

He is the notorious self-appointed rebel in defence circles. President Simba asked Caleb to arrange a one-on-one meeting and dreaded the awaiting hostility. His belly responded to his feelings with rumbling noises.

"Why do I feel so nervous and nauseous? I am the President and this guy kicks the hell out of my sins?" He hissed.

Simba was edgy as he paced up and down in the library. Daniel wanted the meeting to be over, he decided to have it at Kush house on his own terms and home turf.

"Hey, boss, what's up, how is the jungle out there" Daniel welcomed his Defence Minister casually.

Defence Minister Mobo gave his President a salute; took off his coat and sat down. The atmosphere turned ice cold as the two men adjusted in their seats.

"I am concerned about the recent incident in Kano, what happened Mobo? I thought we agreed we should get a briefing before you carry out any operations. Murdering people is contrary to my strategy and beliefs."

"I am not a killer and there is no reason to go around killing our own people. They are helpless people. The last concern for them is voting when their children have no food, water and shelter." Daniel's eyes turned fiery red.

"They prefer the opposition party which means the Members of Parliament must be working hard in that area. I do not look at them as opposition, they are Kushians first, then party second."

"Why can we not stop this childish, immature politics of feuds? I am sick of all this hatred. The problem I have is this_ it's the ordinary people that suffer. I have seen them dance, sing, ululate come rain or sunshine. What's the reward for them, nothing….. Just messing around with them like some computer game? This circus has to stop."

"Listen, Mr President, I do not know how you came to be in power. I have warned you before, the truth shall come out. You cannot fool people anymore. Money will never keep you here forever, you hear me!!..... Who is your financier, I have been watching you, it's time power comes back to its rightful heirs."

Mobo's jugular vein was visibly throbbing and his stern look showed a total revulsion of his President.

"Harvard… my foot!!......where did your poor peasant father get the money to put you through Harvard? Answer me Daniel."

Mobo was seething as he paced up and down the Library as if he was searching for a lost diamond. The corner of his mouth filled with white froth from his saliva. Daniel's sat on his chair without flinching.

"I do not want to waste time answering you. Mobo you should know that many of us got sponsorship from the missionaries. Go to Harvard, check my credentials and my philanthropy here at home."

"Even though I am not of the liberation era; I am a child of this soil as much as you are. This is my promised land as much as the next 15 million Kushians. Whom do you want to rule? Your friends I suppose."

"Simba as long as you continue to sit on this chair you will hear of more atrocities, all with a stamp of your approval. I have done it before, I will continue to do it until you resign. You killed President Zorro and you shall die by the same route."

"Mobo I will not stand here and let you speak such evil. I am not going to waste my breath and talk to a man that has no respect for my office. You can kill us while you are at it. You are a vicious, vindictive, sad, self-centered, selfish person. You have all the blood of those innocent people that you killed on your hands."

Mobo rose and came close to Daniel, nearly hitting him with a good left-hand and stopped himself. Daniel stood still and composed himself and looked Mobo right in the eyes.

"Mobo…with such passion my friend, it is best we use it to make Kush better. Why should we delve into, what and how? That's history let's make a future out of all this mystery then our kids can do better. Mobo, please compose yourself, go home and think about the future."

"I have no regret of my past. It's the future which is our kids, our old age and our families that I am concerned about. Go home Mobo and come back when you ready to uplift Kush."

"We will talk when you are ready to listen. For now I am a spent horse and my spirit is low. I feel sick."

Daniel walked to the nearest waste paper basket and trumpeted his breakfast.

"Are you okay Daniel? Mr President. Wow! You have taken it to heart. Use this tissue." Mobo helped Simba to the chair and they both looked exhausted.

Simba pressed his secret button under the desk for his adviser, and Caleb walked in.

"Mr President you look sick… what has just happened, are you okay?"

Caleb quickly took the basket and shoved it in the next toilet. When he came back Mobo was gone it seemed he had left in a hurry, his coat was still on the hanger.

"No fusing Caleb, I am fine it is just a demonstration of how I feel about that man. He is vile and full of hatred."

"Mr President that was a powerful revelation of his character. You need a goodnight's sleep, it should take care of the foul taste."

Motherland

Kush stretches on a vast land of beautiful diverse scenery on the majestic African continent. The humidity and intense heat in the middle of summer. The contrast of the cool and gentle breeze at night; gives it a mystical character easy to enjoy in one visit.

The well travelled Kushians call winter season their winter. They say it's meant not to upset the people from the colder regions. The Kush winters are mild and short. The winter frost attacks the plants and vegetation in a space of one week. Many plants dry up to prepare for the coming spring.

One can drive through, a hilly and mountainous scenic view and suddenly find oneself in thick and dense foliage. In a few seconds, one can see the open veld of grasslands with wild animals grazing. The next minute one can see zebras, buffaloes and giraffes grazing. Monkeys and rabbits frolicking and the predators setting the laws of the jungle. Tourists recognise the unique aura among the animals in the game parks and safari camps. The animals are at home in game reserves, their natural habitat which has less tampering from humans.

The visitors to Kush say its beauty is an experience of feeling. Kush is a must visit place to come and ensemble the diverse scenery.

One is bound to go back home with an Aha moment.

It's the mystery the aura and its easy-going innocent people ready to greet everyone they meet. Kushians are friendly and always greet you with kind words asking after your health and those that you left behind.

The greeting takes a while; especially with those they know. After the meeting visitors know about the state of affairs of any relatives, good and bad news. The greeting tradition has not changed despite the coming in of telephones and mobile phones. Visiting one another in Kush, one rarely needs to make an appointment. The extended family is ready to welcome visitors.

Kushians have a beautiful culture of sharing even the little food they have. Mothers are creative with cooking and make sure there is food available for visitors from near, far and wide. Pumpkins, sweet potatoes, roasted peanuts and many delicious wild fruits. Chickpeas, groundnuts are snacks, a ready treat for those passing by or visiting.

Husbands look for a wife said to have a giving hand before they marry. The wife works hard to provide for the impromptu visits from friends and family. It's this beautiful camaraderie that many do not get to know about Kush. In the cities, they have it tough but they do try to keep the home pots filled with food to entertain their friends and visitors. In the rural areas, some Kushians travel on foot to their villages.

They can get a place to stay, eat and sleep even in a stranger's home.

Visiting Kush is like a journey back to basics where one meets with nature uninterrupted, as the extravagant companion. The crux of the experience is the vibrant colours, sounds, appearance and its people. The humbleness, trusting and welcoming nature of its people is part of the culture.

Any time is tea time in Kush; no one is in a hurry. Time takes care of its self. This culture has permeated into business practice, a forewarning to visitors is necessary before their coming. They have to be in slow motion like the bionic man and woman. That way they have to stay a little bit longer and enjoy the Kush variety show. Visitors must know it's not worth it to be meticulous. When coming as a tourist do not plan too much. The Kushian will tell you..... *"Akuna Matata."* Meaning no worries tomorrow is another day.

Tourists come to Kush for its simple array of wildlife and natural virgin land which the animals still enjoy without much human meddling. Wild meat called biltong and the exquisite handbags, and belts made from animal hides are a tourist favourite in Kush. Four-by-four trucks, jeeps and helicopters give the fun-loving visitors a taste of life in a Kush animal paradise. Foreign hunters have regulated access to wildlife and make trophies out of their bounty.

The hotels and chalets are of international standards to accommodate the tourists. Kush gives any tourist an experience that lingers for years to come.

Kush has plenty mineral reserves of all kinds; Gold, emeralds, platinum, uranium, diamonds and pits of ore and copper. Earnings from the riches are the exploits of business people who have the means to mine and sell to overseas companies. Lack of foreign investment in manufacturing has deprived this metal-rich country of using their wealth. Kushians work mainly in the underground mines and in clerical jobs. A few Kush professionals join the multinational companies in engineering, accounting and human resources jobs.

The rest are in quasi-government companies and public sector. With a population of around fifteen million people according to the last census, Kush is still a growing nation.

Lion Kings

President Daniel Simba at fifty years old took over after the death of President Liberty Zorro. The First Black President of Kush. The year 1975 is the birth of Kush Republic, after a protracted battle for cry freedom and hearts and minds, it became a free country. Now Sixty years old; Daniel has a youthful appearance and looks young by Kushian standards. With a well-shaved moustache and athletic built, his friends call him a mean machine. Three times a week in the morning, Daniel wakes up early for his regular five mile run across the Kush State House.

His entourage of security details following in pursuit. He is a partial vegetarian and particular about his nuts, grains, fibres and fruit and veg smoothie diets. Daniel drinks more than one litre of water a day and is fond of detoxifying, taking colon cleansers and fasting every quarter.

Daniel lectured his staff that a stomach is a small god and when one eats, it's a temporary bliss. Daniel says he is sure that when people eat, the blood rushes to the stomach in aid of the taxing digestion. When one fasts, the blood rushes to the brain. Daniel fasted before his exams and was adamant his mind was so sharp and alert compared to when he is full.

A healthy athletic man, and could easily pass for forty without any makeover meddling. With no signs of ageing he indeed has put many of his contemporaries to shame.

The more Daniel thought about Caleb's idea, the better it appeared.

"I cannot even imagine it, me, going undercover checking out all the government departments, how am I to pull off such a move. First it's taboo in my culture for a man to wear women's clothes even if it's for disguising purposes. It's a political massacre of the worst kind."

"Are you aware that I am a leader of a country? The psychological effect on children without fathers is unbelievable. The young accept the model we present and are easily impressionable. It's like I am rubber-stamping."

"How will they know it's you when you are undercover?" Caleb was getting irritable.

"My people will burn me at the stake, no matter how noble my intentions are."

Dan paced around the office in deep thought and went to sit in his chair. After much deliberation, Daniel scratched his head and he took his diary.

"I need to sleep over this and mull over it. This is one of the dumbest ideas I have ever heard in my life."

"Surely they say desperate times require desperate measures, I never thought it included me in a dress. Why should we put more fuel into a burning building? Kush is on fire we cannot conceptualise who we are and now it has come to this. Really"

"Caleb what has come over you? How did you come up with such a lame, though fascinating movie script? Allow me to laugh my lungs out. It's hilarious."

****

The next day Daniel was in a mellow mood and seemed to have thought issues through. Caleb, his advisor, was in the office catching up on the daily briefings.

"Caleb, I know there is no way we can do it without a woman's disguise. People will easily sniff me out if I just wear man's clothes."

"I will need a makeover Caleb, like Mrs Doubtfire it is going to be hilarious. Ooh!!... What a load of mambo jumbo comedy." Daniel stood up abruptly.

"Caleb can you imagine me snooping on my ministers and my local government. It's genius; especially visiting my humble electorate the rural masses. They have been patriotic and determined. They are not knowledgeable like our clever townspeople who analyse politician's rhetoric."

Daniel was in stitches as he pondered over this adventure, which to him could easily have been a fantasy story or a kid's adventure in cartoon land. He kept pacing up and down scratching his head at times just laughing to himself.

"I can expound a philosophy of the X and Y chromosome. It's because we have abrogated our responsibilities to the women and we need to reconnect with our X and Y self-being."

"God gave man both genetic carrying genes. The man got the power, we determine the sex of the foetus. Why are we undermining this great accolade given to man? A woman has XX chromosome and man has both XY."

"Where are you going with this expose? Sir, you are really thinking things through. The good night sleep must have helped."

"Seriously though Caleb, if men remain as we are, without getting involved in domestic issues and taking part in raising our kids; our future is bleak. That is the compassionate X chromosome spirit we need to use to solve the state of Kush."

"If we do not loathe dirt and never think of making basic items for our own use. Then I surely would put on a dress and walk the walk than talk the talk."

"We the men have so much we can do to make our women's lives better."

"In the kitchen inventing new gadgets, tools for cutting firewood, strong material for housing and then we can allow our women to beautify themselves as our queens."

"Reproduction becomes a duty because it is tiring; no time for sprucing up as she serves hand over foot and nine months pregnant."

"Hey....Mr President, I like your take on this issue. Surely we already have the X chromosome. Therefore, it needs an awakening to seek excellence, cleanliness, order, and better ways of living. It's the pursuit of the good life and happiness."

"Not pursuit of poverty, dirt and sadness."

Caleb could not contain his excitement seeing how the President was putting the undercover saga into perspective.

"Caleb if enlightenment will take putting on a dress to get democracy bring it on. If it takes an undercover sting operation to get to the truth, let freedom reign. If it takes a wig to get to know a woman's ways, let the games begin." Simba's laugh echoed in the vast library.

During the night, President Simba found himself battling with his conscience. The current dream was pestering him, the same scene. It has little kids with piercing eyes begging for help. The kids look abused, hungry, sick, lonely and lost.

Daniel can not do anything to stop it. It is the same children with the same screaming voices. Such moments made him sweat profusely because he can not save not even one child from the abyss. The children trust him but he is restrained by a great force. Since his coming into Kush house, this dream has not stopped.

Daniel increased his morning jogging miles to clear his mind hoping to get some deep sleep. These children symbolised a great awakening which he could not deal with by himself.

Daniel knew he needed help to understand the meaning of the dream.

****

The current political climate in Kush was now an issue of the people's wish to realise their freedom from colonial rule. Kushians hoping to self-realise through better-managed communities.

The Health and Education Ministries were outsourcing to private enterprises. Kushians in turn finding it difficult to pay the free market prices and excessive charges.

Kushians were now leaving the country to go abroad and find a semblance of normalcy. The global village opened its gates for people to travel, mix and mingle, tasting different systems of governance.

The question that hounded Kushians was why they cannot have a free and fair election without violence and intimidation. Mature politics with goodwill gestures from every party. Guns and bloodshed were the only product seen on the streets in Kush after elections. The ordinary people hack one another to death if they disagree. Force marching and killing if they try to stay put in their homesteads.

After the independence of Kush, ordinary Kushians were struggling as they did during colonial rule. They were failing to find an easier life through government impetus and committed development projects.

****

The late President Liberty Zorro was the first black President of Kush, known as a man of the people. He won the elections with a ninety percent majority vote. His vision was to lift the people of Kush from poverty and slowly create vibrant communities. Zorro was keen to set up cooperative projects and micro financing aimed at small businesses. His aim was to create an active culture within the communities and local business involvement.

Universities and college students were expected to volunteer on attachments, the rewards becoming an investment for the future. This was Zorro's vision.

Zorro encouraged the people through volunteering programmes to gain business experience. With the local government overseeing activities by giving incentives.

A charity centred community, Zorro thought could bring people together; instead of just focusing on monetary rewards. He reminded the people how early colonial settlers had the privileges and legacies from their ancestors in the developed world. Zorro wanted Kushians to have a starting point and develop a base for their future in their settled land. He addressed his people.

"Remember from history, champions of democracy started as small general dealers. This enterprising spirit became a success story of the corporate giants which became global brands.

These ventures are the Mc-Do and Mc-Can brands they are everywhere. We also need our own Mc-Kush brands to become a Continental brand. Forget international, because they will give you a fair trade logo." Zorro urged his people.

Focus on your continent of Africa, he urged the young people. It should be acceptable that a Kushian starts small; learn the business shrewdness and advance.

Don't despair, because of the progress of fully developed economies with theories that do not refer to your destination, start small." Zorro bellowed to his people.

The United Corporations was getting weary of Zorro's rhetoric. The government's inner circle was getting nervous with his open and robust vision of a self-sufficient Kush. United Corporation saw his vision as counterproductive to a One-World Vision.

Zorro on one of his Africa League visits which he chaired he had negated the principles advanced by the United Corporations.

"What we need is Africa as an equal player on the global market; not aid or grants, that's a beggar's bowl."

Kushians were expecting change and still struggling. Zorro went ahead with the Economic Structural Adjustment Programme, to allow free market systems to run. Kush could only access financial packages to refinance the national debt inherited from colonial rule; after the proposed changes.

This eventually defeated Zorro's noble intentions. Kushians saw this as a beggar cannot be choosers' game.

President Liberty Zorro being the first president had a lot to prove to his people. He would say,

"This is not civilisation, we are the leaders allowing our people to suffer. Leaders are not showing the people a good vision, we are busy looking for our own good life. A hungry man is an angry man, an international relations policy tool used since men knew how to abuse power.

****

President Daniel Simba and his Vice President Dumbo found time to reminisce on this great man of the soil. President Zorro had charted a way for them into office.

"Bless President Zorro and his socialist heart; he had his priorities in the right place. He did not know what hit him. Slapped with sanctions by the big guns they all started pulling out their investments.

The big fish made a clear message that they mean business. Zorro had to tour the line no matter the cost to the general population." Daniel found inspiration in this great man of Kush.

"It's sad though Dumbo; Zorro was a true patriot and a son of the soil. Zorro got a golden handshake. He refused and got slapped with an Economic Structural Adjustment Programme with repayment terms, bang out of order. It is like selling the country."

"The Chinese came like knights in shining armour only to further worsen the situation. We inherited a bankrupt economy which was economically engineered Dumbo, it was an election advantage for us."

"In came Captain Planet in the form of you Daniel Simba. Nothingness rising to something. They believe in us Daniel they do, even when the state of the nation is worse off. They think Zorro tried and bit more than he could chew."

"The saddest thing is the way our own children appear on international media. I do not like watching the poverty adverts when I am abroad. It's a time when my conscience nudges me and say."

'Hey… how are you doing, enjoying your life, is this the good life and pursuit of happiness?"

"I feel like I am not human Dumbo, we are the fathers and should be responsible nationally for all our children. Just basic things like water, food, shelter and clothing.

It is like we have abrogated our responsibilities to the international community."

****

The sudden death of President Zorro came as a shock to all the Kushians. The government set a week of national mourning, the flag was flying at half-mast. Condolence messages were pouring into the country.

The United Corporations sent a message with a promise to help the country to move on. They pledged financial support to allow the country not to fall back into recession and tribal wars.

The chairperson of United Corporations spoke passionately on national TV of their unwavering support. He stressed their willingness to supply military forces and peacekeepers to deter guerrilla insurgencies. They reported the death of Zorro to be sinister workings of radical war militants, wanting to destabilise Kush.

Kush had enjoyed peace after the war of freedom. Scuffles were mainly from disgruntled opposition members and politicians who felt disenfranchised.

President Zorro was a practical man he tried to build national unity and reconciliation. He thanked every tribe and allowed everyone to express their anxieties and their hopes of a new Kush.

He had outdone his contemporaries by being non-partisan when addressing his people. Zorro agreed to have a constitution and welcomed the nation's contribution with enthusiasm. Kushian values and beliefs; Zorro listened.

He was passionate about his country and showed wisdom by making sure schools teach local languages in all provinces to foster cohesion and national unity.

On his inauguration Zorro a proud son of Kush declared.

"I Liberty Zorro, do declare that by the powers vested in me by the people of Kush. I will serve this beautiful nation of Kush without fear or favour."

"My mandate is to govern Kush, not on tribal lines. Therefore as your humble servant and by God's grace. I will serve the wonderful people of this nation. God bless Kushians and God bless the Republic of Kush."

Zorro never stooped low to allow tribal affiliations to fester in his cabinet. It was breaking news on national TV that President Zorro during question time he summarily dismissed a Member of Parliament called Smoko. It was because of his divisive rants and tribal partisan bickering. Zorro told him,

"Young man if you want to talk tribal, this is not the place and time. Go find a cave and do your bickering. This is Kush Cabinet deciding Kush business not cave dwellers politics. Get your hairy body out of here, turn back the clock. While you are at it, go make some bows and arrows and start your own tribal wars."

It was a full house applause, everyone on their feet awakened to this new leadership.

The message was loud and clear, no one could play child politics with Zorro he wanted mature politics.

"Ask yourself; what have I done today to make my country proud."

It was Zorro's last quote after every meeting. Visibly fuming Zorro walked out of the meeting, they had to adjourn to another date.

He always challenged each Member of Parliament to go and visit their constituency and talk to the people not party faithful only. Zorro wanted his Cabinet to know the real issues affecting the people rather than passing the buck, wasting time with concubines in luxury hotels. He became notorious for firing lazy Members of Parliament who did not do well in their jobs. Zorro asked Cabinet Ministers to declare their expenses publicly.

Some cabinet ministers had no experience in running ministries they got the majority votes; despite the little education they have. With no experience, the progress in many government departments was minimal.

Sango, the minister of health, was proactive he was passionate about his job and took a keen interest in his responsibility. What frustrated him most was the permanent secretary's doodling on health policies.

He was indifferent and in a world of his own private business. Sango wanted a general provision of malaria tablets and mosquito nets provided free in rural areas.

He recommended 'water is life' programme by getting boreholes dug in remote villages but received a lukewarm response.

On his visit to an opposition stronghold, he was booed by angry villagers telling him to go back and spend his millions while singing

"Do a body count Sango wants to dig some graves."

The village chief fervently swore on his grandfathers' life that it was a curse. He urged the people to visit the witch doctors especially seeing the convulsions caused by the fever.

Minister of Agriculture Kano is a college dropout. He knew nothing about farming and grew up in a crowded tower block in Edom notorious for crime. A clever man and knows his territory in and out. Local voters in Edom were afraid of Kano; they would rather vote in fear than face his intimidation. Kano had no clue what the nation needed to aid the agricultural based economy.

Kushians are willing to work but the government's spirit is lacking. Kano was not a team player and solely depended on his deputy to run the show.Kushians expect the government to help them with farming technology and initial start-up capital.

The government does not have enough resources to microfinance projects. Loans and finance issues are the jurisdiction of foreign banks. International banks want collateral a condition the masses cannot meet. The government does not have enough funds to help Kushians.

The masses did not want to look back in history to the memories of colonial rule. The journey to freedom was a painful and scarring experience.

Fortunate Kushians who were in the right place at the right time felt the struggle for independence was just a fad. The economic pie was not enough for the 15 million people scrambling to get a piece of food, shelter, and clothing, just basic needs.

Employment opportunities are mostly in quasi-government companies, which are parastatals and local government. The influx of graduates fill in these posts, in telecoms, electricity supply authorities and some mineral marketing corporations and grain marketing boards.

Kushians dreamt of working in their own factories and mines and other business ventures. Kushians wondered who was in charge; government or international community. Kushians lost families in the struggle for independence and many lost their children.

President Zorro extended a hand of friendship to every citizen so that Kush could move on. Kushian women and children bore the brunt of the scuffles that happen in the country. When elephants mate the grass suffers the chiefs used to say. This is how the women felt when men decided to fight, kill, do dirty politics and start wars. It's the women who were looking forward to a change in Kush. They expected a new dawn to usher in a new era. For Kushians: for the people by the people.

Corruption Fever

As President Daniel Simba took over the reins of power from the late President Zorro, the information technology system was a disaster and mishmash of different international countries' expertise. More than ten International companies bid for the digital telephone exchange tenders, each finding a portion of the country to showcase their knowledge. The digital telephone system was not compatible nationally. Each bidding country's specifications could not merge to connect with the national digital exchange. The government had to abandon the projects several times.

The poor Kushians innocently celebrated waiting for better phone systems not realising that it is going to be a long call to freedom. A unified single digital exchange project with a potential for national roll over was the initial plan before greed got in the way. Alas, many greedy hands wanted to make sure they get a piece of the digital wires for their own pockets. The extent of the corruption involved possible human heckling and elimination as the digital telephone race had become a gravy boat.

The brilliant young Kush technicians were the ones to pick up the wires and make sense of the digital mess, created by the greedy ministers not interested in national glory and computerised visions.

The winners of this mishmash corporate greed money were the ministers and the dotting international corporations.

With the struggling national budget, information technology programmes were going to put a strain on many ministerial government budgets. Caleb was adept at computer technology, he felt irritable when he could not access online sites without frequent interruption.

Kush government was slow in training staff in Information Technology. Caleb urged his President to be proactive and push every department to be compliant with latest computer technology. He knew that any delay in incorporating the new technology could be futile and render Kush obsolete on the international scene. The various ministerial departments came up with all sorts of financial plans and the cost of computerisation seemed beyond reach. Kushians want to realise change; yet the fiscal is struggling, the fast paced technology was crippling every progress.

It was a well-known fact that professionals were leaving the country in thousands. Doctors, teachers and nurses. Kush country was training for the Diaspora and Daniel felt helpless and could not do anything about it.

"Kushians are emigrating, I cannot keep them. I cannot competitively pay them. Poverty and corruption reign for those that remain while I am in a fix about whose loyalty I serve.

It's the brave and daring people who have stayed in Kush to keep up appearances in their own country."

"Few have been smart and played the game through hardships, with a little bribe here, hard work there, they have done well. Some Kushians are doing well in the Diaspora, realising their dreams and actualizing themselves. That's what life should be." Daniel always reminded his adviser Caleb.

Daniel and Maya preferred to have their children educated abroad and always knew how his own sons felt about home politics. He would at times question his decisions.

"Maya, Kushians must wonder why we send our kids abroad for education when I am the president. It is playing double standards" Dan would talk to his wife, Maya.

"Dan you are not the first and last president to do this practice. There is no justification for doing this, though, honey. The best education is from international universities, they are not in Africa."

Daniel's son Abel once told him that even with the privileges they have; there was something about the ethics, philosophy, virtues and community spirit of the Diaspora. Everyone mucking in, politicians, locals, professionals and never afraid to get their hands dirty. Daniel was proud of his sons. They told him that despite being rich they just fitted in with everybody whether rich or mediocre.

Abel reminded his father about Kush culture where one has to put a privilege badge on the forehead so everybody knows it before you tell them.

"Dad there is no humility in our bravado arrogance and loudness."

Abel held part-time jobs as an unpaid intern at a London law firm and worked in restaurants just to create his resume.

"No one cares about whom we are Papa. I am free in a foreign land." Abel reminded his Pa.

"It's a better way to live than the excessively rich licking culture in Kush." Jude is the quiet one, he never had much to say.

Daniel thought how privileged he was to afford his children a good education. After spending his University years in the States, Daniel knew about the temptations that young people face when studying abroad. His sons had not yet been caught up in a life of opulence and reckless lifestyle.

It's the other millions of children in Kush that might go without reading and writing.

Kushians toiled day and night and are proud of their country. Of late the economic strain was ripping through the moral fibre of every decent man and woman. It was hard going, even with basics like bread.

Kushian mothers sought means to make bread at home they had to bribe wholesalers and suppliers. Bread a staple food, for lunch boxes, home meals it was getting hard to just get by.

Fuel queues are in every garage, people bribing to get a few litres. The passport office cashes in on the act; a haven for palm greasing and the issue is the chain of corruption from top to bottom. The officers were getting crafty asking for bribes to just refer someone to the person that could get the passport done. Kushians were now leaving the country in droves and dozens. Getting a passport is a big-time business for the corrupt officers.

President Simba was unaware of the corruption within his cabinet and how it was filtering down to the grassroots level. Churches, charities tried to preach and make TV programmes but to no avail. Church leaders spoke the same message, the locals could not find an alternative to help themselves. Kushians fund themselves stuck between a rock and hard place.

Short-term indulgence moved in, ethics and virtues were seen flying out of many government and business windows.

Tel Mobile, a domestic telecoms company, tried to remain bold and invested in Kush. Tel Mobile won an award for a best telecoms provider in the year 2000 to become a number one job search site on the continent.

The year 2001 saw the protracted legal battle pursued by the government and the company had to pack up shop and go abroad. 'Black on black fighting', the financial newspaper reported.

The University students wrote to the government complaining that a beacon of African enterprise is taken out of business. Kush local businesses found it difficult to be self-reliant without the help of the government and bank capital.

The government was silent, economists and relevant departments were mum about this issue.

Soul Searching

Daniel sat in the secret garden most summer evenings to ponder on the problems hounding the nation. The tranquillity and fresh air from the nearby lake was very calming. The lavenders rose bushes, lilies, carnations, chrysanthemums, gardenias and hydrangeas are a florist's treasure trove on this Presidential State House.

"Honey it's getting cold out there come inside, Maya called out."

"Why don't you come out and sit with me in the fresh air. It's therapeutic darling." Maya obliged.

"Ohm you smell lovely honey, which perfume. It's the one I bought, I think?" Daniel rose to give Maya a peck on the cheek.

"No darling it's Abel, he is a copycat, and he has become a man of fine taste," Maya answered as she stared intensely at Daniel.

"Looking forward to your holiday Honey? Daniel gave Maya a gentle squeeze.

"Oh yes! School holidays can be manic but an escape to Malaysia is what I need, it is beautiful, the spa and beauty treatments. Daniel, you look distant, what is on your mind why are you not joining us for the holidays,"

"Honey, Maya I told you I am going on a working holiday within and without"

Maya put a glass of juice on the side table and a tray of Hors d'oeuvre.

"Dan, why don't you share the details with me, I am your confidante honey, why are you hushed up" Maya moved closer and rested her head on Daniel's shoulder.

"No Maya, not until I meet with the security team; it is top secret. I cannot say much at the moment wifey."

"But Honey, Maya, honestly tell me, what do you think about our country? Are we doing the right things or are we not just a bunch of sell-outs, a messed up cabinet concerned with our pockets than service." Daniel sat looking in the distance.

"You said it dear, I didn't." Maya answered with a cold tone.

"Are we not going to answer for the inhuman treatment, the poor kids' adverts, the divisions on tribal lines? Tribalism is one of the most stupid conflict instruments ever propagated since man's existence. I find it so trivial."

"If I was a tribal man, I do not think I could have made it at Harvard because all I saw were people different from me." Daniel kept talking.

"Honey I am yet to see and hear us address our people solely as the leaders of a country without bringing tribe or partisan politics into it, it's pathetic. Tribalism will continue to keep us in chains and make us fail to reach our full potential Honey."

"We cannot escape from the party structures that's the order of nations. It's you the leaders that promote it externally instead of using it as your internal audit tool for management purposes. When you stand on the podium, you are addressing Kushians not party faithful."

"Dan dear, it started in the Bible from creation, remember the 12 tribes of Israel. Christ is the lion of the tribe of Judah. Honey, the distinction was not to promote wars and infighting; these tribes clearly showed the different qualities of men."

"I am not talking about having a Utopia on earth. It's to realise the diverse nature of man and still see that we are from one Creator."

"Benjamites were murderers and they met consequences of their actions. Track their ancestry you will see the implications of their legacy from their descendants."

"Check genealogy of the rest of the tribes. Some showed wisdom and artisanship. Study the legacy of each tribe then you will have answers to our own existence; we need to break the curse by loving ourselves first honey before anyone can respect us."

"We can still live together despite the differences."

"I agree Maya that is an interesting take on the subject. Daniel picked a glass of juice and drank noisily.

"You are slurping Daniel again, stop it, you will embarrass us one day on national TV if you make it a habit."

"Come on Maya, when am I ever going to be me and gulp my drink, dunk my biscuit, rub my nose, and scratch my crotch without someone calling the fashion police. Please give me some space to be me, without the media taking me to pieces. Let a man live in peace for once."

"Very well Mr President your wishes are my command" Maya playfully stroked Daniel's lap.

Daniel rarely burdened his wife with sensitive issues or any intricate details from the government circles. He seemed eager to just express himself today which was rare.

Culturally a Kushian man is a breadwinner. If they are issues raised the man has to tackle them in silence. Skeletons in the cupboard come out, on the day the family head dies. During funerals, it's the time to know the members of the clan. Stepsisters and Stepbrothers and the real firstborn and mistresses too. Fathers who die intestate, the funeral at times can be a hilarious occasion. The father's shenanigans come home to roost on the day big daddy kicks the bucket.

The firstborn discovers that he is not the eldest, when big brother shows up at big dad's funeral.

At times an intestate will, can bring brawls and commotions when the dotting ever-present wife discovers that a genuine, legitimate distant remote controlled wife and children were just looming in the countryside unnoticed. Such a situation can easily become a film-maker's paradise. Women are expected to have a quiet spirit and agree with whatever the house head says.

"It's still a man's world in Kush." Daniel fumed.

Daniel was a reformed man, the Diaspora renaissance changed his views on marriage. He adored his wife without being apologetic and felt a calm spirit when they are together. Daniel saw in his childhood days many homes in the village with polygamous marriages.

The elders said the women are cantankerous and talk like persistent raindrops on a tin roof. Bickering, hollering and scuffles are a constant affair. His father did not follow the cultural norm to marry many wives.

He argued that just being with one is enough homework he can never finish and pass.

Daniel liked Maya's calm spirit, her philosophy was never to argue in front of the children. When Daniel felt the urge to shout, Maya told him to use sign language. She did not want negative energy brought into the house. Daniel took refuge in the secret garden and at times in their study room.

Once in a while they had a no holds barred family meeting. At the meeting, they could talk about family issues which need ironing out.

Each family member could say whatever they have done during the week without facing repercussions. These meetings brought them closer and the children knew that they could make mistakes and get family advice and protection.

The kids realised they were normal and that their parents went through the same growing pains. Daniel adored Maya, they were friends first and a couple second. Dan always said,

"I will classify everyone by how they contribute to my life's path. My children are my mirror."

****

Daniel's father is a peasant farmer a man of good repute and one wife. In the village it is a normal occurrence to hear families with many concubines squabbling and fighting; the main reason being jealousy and poverty. During the colonial reign it was hard for many families to explore new opportunities, the government checked the indigenous native's movements and tried to control their welfare.

The majority of Kushians were settled in the tribal trust lands where facilities are just basic. Men with many wives they have many children. Children become extra labour for chores to work the land and home duties.

The man's job is mainly to be the head and go around the compound, commanding his family to his best interest.

Daniel's family was stable, and the father a hard-working peasant farmer. His mother, the queen of the kitchen and no one, can challenge her in that area, they all knew it.

Sara, Daniel's sister complained.

"Mum I wish people can stop eating forever then you will not be so cranky and bullying; *Baleboste* that's what you are."

"What!!, Bala who? Sara's mum quizzed her.

"Its Yiddish mum you will never understand."

"Don't speak no gibberish to me young lady, you are getting too much knowledge from these English schools. Now you are speaking in tongues have you joined the evangelical churches too? Argh! Do your dishes now!"

She screamed brandishing a besom in her hand.

"Continue with your insolence, and scrub the floor while you are at it" she shouted back.

Daniel followed his father around the farm to learn skills to keep the homestead going. He learnt how to repair the fences and how to deliver the sheep babies and cows. The kitchen was no man's land. Daniel Simba's domain was in the fields and grazing areas with his cows, sheep and goats.

In the valley, Daniel sat down like a good shepherd and watched the sheep graze while he took many holidays to many countries in one book or another. He had pen pals that sent him books from abroad and a selection from Mills and Boom, Shakespeare to John Grisham and biographies of many world changers like Lee Iacocca.

This solitude was a blessing in disguise as he felt there was more to life than just land and cows. There Daniel dreamt of a life far away from the maddening women and farm animals.

****

As Daniel and Maya sat in the garden enjoying the birds playing the evening orchestra epilogue. The sun was slowly beginning to descend into the horizon with a shimmering bright orange flame.

"But honey, why are our young people going on a rampage killing their families as well. The chief commander told me the young brigades, the green bombers, went to the villages."

"They ransacked and burnt the poor huts to the ground. Many innocent people have died accused of not voting for me in the last elections. Maya, I never sent anyone to do such a thing this is a mutiny?" Daniel carried on with his deep thoughts.

"One thing I have known from my culture which I always believed in, is the way we used to regard human life. If a family member is killed. The community used to treat such acts with disgust, the perpetrators became outcasts."

"The whole village treated murderers with contempt, it was enough punishment, darling to go through with such rejection."

"This strategy by the defence minister is cruel and rampant. What heritage is this, using young minds and our future generation?"

"Desperate young boys are now ransacking villages and cities on a killing spree; it is just contrary to what we believe in, the sanctity of human life."

"Are we becoming immune to human pain, suffering and death? This culture is a recipe for poverty, wars and destabilisation. Once upon a time it was a rare occurrence to hear of someone's death. We were a peaceful people, content with what we have and hard-working. Tell me darling am I responsible as President. Will I be accountable in the later life?"

Daniel was now holding his hands to his face and looking dejected he started moving his body up and down as if doing the mantras.

"Honey, are you okay, you are scaring me, what's with you these days. Is someone after you? Do they want you out Daniel, you gone all spiritual on me?"

"I told you to watch your army commander he thinks he is invincible and seems not to take you seriously. How many times has he defied your directives and done something else."

"He clearly shows contempt to you, even in public. Are those tears in your eyes? You worrying me Daniel" Maya looked intently with sad eyes towards her husband."

"It's not about Mobo darling, no. Maya that's why I avoid having deep thoughts with you. If we the leaders do not reflect and look back and see whether we are doing the right things then I have no conscience."

Maya put her hand on her husband's lap.

"Honey, the situation with Kush is more complex than our people know. You try to do the right things and the invisible powers will find a way to upset every policy, and ideologies you can advance, to micro-manage Kush to a bigger picture or entity."

"The once proud Kushians are like beggars everywhere, here and abroad. Today I saw our people dancing, drumming and wiggling their bottoms in Europe trying to get visas to stay. The young and old."

"Instead of getting angry it nudged my mind. I asked myself what I am doing in my position when my people, my own Kushians are leaving the country. What are we doing wrong, why are we allowing them to go and work in menial roles."

"Every channel in the West displays our children in most disturbing ways, the charities are begging, pleading for money and sponsors to help our own children." Daniel started to weep helplessly.

"Honey you need to get a grip you knew what you bargained for, to become sheep in wool's clothing and dance a foreign tune instead of our own drums and ululations."

"What's become of us Maya? Mala fide leaders, we are sell-outs. The legal system and politics are all based on foreign economic principles. We cannot correlate ourselves to the economic and political systems we inherited, hence who we have become."

"The old civilisations did no need theories to have strong governments. Capitalism, Socialism that's man's way of creating divisions, classes and conquering." Daniel rarely outpoured with such emotion."

"Bless President Liberty Zorro; he wanted so much to Africanise Kush he said it, and what happened to him? He believed in our national sovereignty."

Maya, he said this to me on our wedding night.

"Young man, it's not too late for you intellectuals to sit down and drive forward a Kush economic agenda. Write a Kush report on good governance and best practice.

We need our own philosophy and ethics. Kush philosophers, sit down have a think tank, be life changers; we need to or else we are a doomed race.

Have terms of reference for the future generation. You cannot keep referring to foreign philosophy because we only have folk tales which are grandpa's tales.

Remove the weak links and revive our heritage. What we have done is causing us to be gullible, so it's now time for plan B. We will remain weak if we do not do something now. Let's push for education policies that promote the young and teach ethics and virtues at an early age.

Encourage team spirit projects and discipline. Kush should become a country of inventors. Not the bumping and grinding with hypnotising music. Our youths have a platform for cussing, gangster music and dancing. Asians are busy swatting and discovering the universe while we are world entertainers. Science and technology is important for us to keep appearances on the International scene. If we do not get inside the motherboard of computers, we will be remote controlled children until heaven comes. Let us implement policies that can make our future generation stronger."

"Zorro was a passionate man he said."

"Africa needs to indigenize its existence, with values and ethics to meet the present and future centuries."

"What can we say is our legacy", Zorro asked,

"It's poverty; bravado, wiggling bottoms, loudness the list goes on." Zorro would say

"Have a vision, children of the soil, change the future, start now. See how proud other nations are; Kushians should be more patriotic."

"Just walk outside and see what our kids are wearing. Its Western gear promoting other countries and Universities. No one wearing a Kush brand. Say no to corruption say no to hatred of one another, say no to tribalism."

This was Zorro's vision which we are undoing now."

Daniel looked animated and starry-eyed as he poured out to his wife.

"Darling Maya, China has distinguished itself despite communism, India, Singapore they are uniquely identifiable as whom they are. For us, it's like there is an invisible controller. I feel a déjà vu, Zorro was like my father, I miss him."

"Daniel, be careful darling if you want to resign the post just tell them and retire safely." Maya fell in love once again, to this man, she married, with much on his shoulder to carry.

"But I committed myself till …Sshh; Okay darling I am getting all muddled up" Daniel corrected himself."

"The kids need to be safe. They are abroad Maya I need them safe, I will just try to be careful and hang on until they finish school and settled. I shall miss you darling enjoy Malaysia." They kissed and held hands until the sun disappeared into the horizon.

Kush House

The grand Kush House stands on a hilly place just outside the city of Edom, overlooking the sprawling city in Kush. Over the years, it has started to lose its vibrancy and glitter. Edom was once a bustling capital with new infrastructure taking space. Makeshift open markets and dilapidated buildings overshadow the once proud city. Squatter camps are sprawling on the city outskirts as mass migration from the villages' increases.

People are looking for any place to put up shelter and try to make a living. Plastic shelters, cupboard, tin, even dry grass, one can find small little spaces with human beings living inside. Little babies shouting and crying announcing their arrival into the world. The government does not know, life goes on as usual in the makeshift homes. No birth certificate no health care no lineage and no heritage just as the animals in the forest. Animals at the Zoo have a better life, Rangers do a stocktake.

Money traders line the streets shouting about their goods. One can find any world currency at alarming rates. The stock market is now just a white elephant as many foreign investors packed up shop. The architecture of the old buildings influenced by the settlers who scrambled for Africa in the early 18th century.

The route to Kush house is an unfolding escapade to a new world order. The gardens and the roads leading to the State House are in mint condition, manicured, no potholes or dusty lanes.

Jacaranda trees serenade the Kush Avenue and in summer it makes a beautiful picture risqué postcard as the purple flowers fall and carpets the pavements. It's a world away from the hustle and bustle of the capital city. The soldiers and police squads dressed neatly in their colonial uniforms are marching with such precision and skill to the delight of the people.

Soldiers and police squads are up and about protecting the first family in Kush. The presidential security shift is a hot potato and intelligence personnel fight over the job because it has an assured payday.

****

Tom Dumbo, the Vice President, came to Kush House for a special briefing. The two presidents were friends before they came into office. They met in Russia were Dumbo was studying his journalism degree. Daniel and Caleb were also taking additional studies in International Relations and Law in Russia. The trio kept the country guessing where the economy was heading.

"Dumbo my dear comrade and friend, I called you here to brief you on a mission I am about to undertake."

"It's top secret; only the coded smart elect will take part. From next week, I am going on holiday. I want you to organise with the media they should know you are taking over. I know of cause you will delegate but you need to hear me out, my friend."

Daniel and Dumbo the two presidents met in Russia before coming into office and their friendship continued.

They went down the stairs to what Daniel calls his secret catacomb. It is a private room with rich and elaborate furniture and more like a study room with mahogany and oak bookshelves. One can find hunter's trophies of Buffalo, Lions, Kudus, Cheetahs and Zebra heads gracing walls of the executive library suit.

"Dumbo my family is going away on holiday to Malaysia at our holiday house. I am happy there won't be any urgent cabinet meetings to do. Its summer holiday season everything will work out. I am asking an independent internal audit team to go undercover. I want to use this internal audit route to know what goes on in my country. I want to know what is going on beneath the Kush surface."

"Are you out of your mind? Daniel, I think it's a bit too far-fetched. Why do you have to go undercover, is intelligence and your personal advisers not telling you enough about the state of the nation?"

"You put me to shame as your deputy that you do not even believe in me and what I share with you. How long have we known each other, from the village we went to the same school?"

"In Russia during our refuge we shared a lot Daniel. We are bound by secrecy this world knows not. Here we are after a protracted battle, we are in power and you doubt the process. The people love us and fear us, what more do you want. You have three mansions overseas. What more Mr President what more do you want? Kiki and Maya are into this new age beauty. They have Spa treatments, liposuctions and Botox enhancements. Lasting beauty" Dumbo was exasperated as he bounced up and down.

Daniel tried to cough.

"Ugh, I do not fancy this new age beauty stuff. Did you get to hear that Bongo's wife died on the operating table? She was getting a __ohm what do they call it, nip and tuck that's it. Why should we change what nature has given."

"Daniel you know how our women are susceptible to big bellies and fibroids, with age, but medical breakthrough does wonders."

"Our people do age gracefully though my friend, they do not need any enhancements look at my Maya."

"Don't be a show-off, it's what we have grown to accept. My wife has to be energetic till death do us part. Why allow the laws of gravity to cause chaos when medical science can do something."

"Maya looks young you know, her body is always fit and natural you are a lucky man Daniel."

"My friend we shop anywhere in the world and get the best medical treatments overseas. Life is good for us, this is a good life Daniel we are chasing happiness."

"You are right my good friend." Daniel agreed.

"Ohm… I have a dental appointment in Hungary in March, they are good at cosmetic dentistry and I need some veneers."

"Daniel you are the president, why not use the local general hospital."

"They do try. Oh, but I do not think they have all the chemicals and proper tools. I cannot take a chance I still have some years left to smile about. I do not want to get infections like hepatitis and gum diseases."

Dumbo came and sat next to Daniel.

"I am happy as Vice President. If I cover for you, the allowance is okay so, *no Matata*."

"That's why I trust you, Dumbo you are loyal and unwavering. Sometimes the conscience has to wake up Dumbo. I just feel that I need to get down to basics and see the places I left thirty years ago. I grew up in a village my family could not afford much. My father was just a peasant farmer."

"I thank the Missionaries at Mase Mission School they sponsored me. I would have amounted to nought. We were selected for a scholarship later, I felt chosen and my destiny set by some force which was unnatural. The way of the world and the freedom we think we have is edited history. It's a well-played Big Brother show of universal appeal, my friend. You know what I mean the things we have to do to keep ourselves where we are." The two Presidents sat and chatted away in this dimly lit library.

"Sshh__ Daniel, the walls have ears you know. Politics is now a filthy, dirty game. Politics is not for the squeamish or weak people. Whatever is happening now was set up 2000 years ago. We are tools rubber-stamping whatever the invisible directs. It's agonising to see politicians of today labour and calculate every word verb and adjective. Politicians have to be savvy with words they say. Why?....... Politics is a game of scrabbled chase."

****

The two presidents set in the basement chuckling and nibbling on Hors d'oeuvre as they sipped on grape juice.

"It's pain-stacking when politics loses sincerity and honesty. It's happening to some today and it can happen to us if we cross the line or become obsolete."

"It's no longer necessary to study about economics, and politics when the world economic joysticks are in the hands of one interest group."

"The media has managed to champion one-world governance through the study of the mind."

"Don't worry Dumbo it's all safe down here in the basement. It's the only place I can have private talks with family and friends without fear of bugging and eavesdroppers.

"Daniel I am too old for these games I just want to be able to live and see my grandchildren grow. I do worry Daniel, about my sanity, how can we live with such a legacy we are creating for our people. Nothing has changed much since we took over."

"My granddad warned me about our generation. He said that we should be changers and not enforcers of Kushian poverty. He said that wars, tribal squeamishness and poverty are shaping the present and the next generations, so he always said love yourselves; your own people. Stop the slave attitude it breeds no civilisation."

"We have allowed ourselves to be used, abused and have fat bank accounts at the end of our reign. With a price of possible impeachment or prison. Where Daniel?"

"At the international court of justice. What a travesty for an African to be tried in an international court of justice. It's laughable my good friend. Daniel, can you imagine them dragging us to that court? I can see you being defiant my friend." Dumbo laughed so loud the walls echoed.

"As long as we do not own the means of production and intellectual property rights it's just a constipated existence. We need to be knowledgeable to invent items for our people. If we try, they say it is someone's patent."

"We should be the ones to motivate and sponsor our kids to do research and development in science and technology. We shall be at the mercy of the International community."

"For freedom to take place, there is a sacrifice, our people tire of never-ending hardships and sacrifices."

"Kushians want to build active communities, we are not there to lead them. We are cocooned, we have tight security just for us. Daniel, we have a fleet of security cars and helicopters everywhere we go. If we have nothing to fear, we should walk on the street freely." Daniel and Tom sat leisurely reminiscing on good old days.

"President Zorro had a vision Dumbo; land back to the people. He always said the world debacle is all about land and Moses was Promised Land, not worthless dollars, but land."

"It's from the beginning that man has sought land and fought over land. He who owns the land rules the rest. Everything we need is from the land and politics strives on land policies."

"This is where we find gold and silver. The journey should have taken a week, Moses circled and lost the way for forty years looking for the Promised Land that must mean something."

"How right he was, because minerals, plants, animals are from the soil. Do not forget that he never got to see the Promised Land. Dumbo, Moses did it for his people, he sacrificed himself. Our people cannot see their promised land as they stand on it because they were placed in sandy barren soil."

"Daniel, the greedy will never rest until all the wealth is gone. Nations with mineral wealth are the ones languishing in poverty how sad. Kush has vast wealth."

"You and I it's all about power my friend, nothing but absolute power which corrupts absolutely so they say."

"Kush people are poor and their dignity is owning a piece of land. The dignity of men is on the land, where we meet with nature uninterrupted, not our city mansions. I find peace when I go to the farm Daniel, just walking in solitude. At the farm, I am energised and stress less."

"Kush has enough land to settle our people and visitors too. There is a need for change. We still use the same minority laws used by the settlers against us. We are not offering the direction and leadership to have civilised communities. We are still in shackles."

"Not us Dumbo. It's the masses, that suffer, it's how we got where we are. We both have mansions and farms, that's the best of both worlds."

"Come rain, hunger or sunshine, Kushians come scantily dressed and dance. When they dance our faces go Humpty-Dumpty on the women's bosoms."

"It's is so touching my friend." The two presidents sat and chatted about their legacy.

"Somehow the rich nations realised the importance of owning land. Remember the scramble for Africa. One person owning vast areas of land. Hence why it's easy for them to still control us because they have vast tracks of land in our own countries."

"Especially the private farms and islands. A lot happens on these privately owned lands and it's usually not good for Kush. Even weapons stashing and funding of rebels.

****

As President Daniel Simba and Vice President Dumbo settled into power, the free market system was now creating a new social and economic order.

Corruption had become endemic and risen to unprecedented proportions. People were taking bribes for flour, bread, passports or anything that is scarce.

The resilience of humanity to survive can easily be typified in Kush. Women are the most creative and ingenious innovators of survival techniques. Cross-border trading, selling at the market anything to keep the kids breathing. People just trod on when babies arrive on Kush soil. Somehow society adapts to this environment as homoeostasis sets its scales. Some Kushians fail to cope and rely on weed and alcohol to waste away.

This is an economy, psychosocially and financially engineered by the new breed of neo-liberals Daniel Simba and Tom Dumbo with the help of their financiers.

The two Presidents could sit for hours in this dim lit and secret chamber. Time sailed on without notice.

"Dumbo that's why I want to use my auditors to go undercover. It's to see why we have such disparities. You have to listen to me Dumbo I am serious."

"Sit down Dumbo, our own children have the finest of things. Abel is at Oxford, Jude is at Harvard, and they own properties overseas. Dumbo we should have this progress at home? We have to see things differently. Our continent is a laughing stock of International Relations, everything negative is about Africa. We have to change Dumbo it's not too late."

"I am tired of these greedy ministers battering, lying about most things to please me. I ask myself Dumbo what legacy are we leaving for our children. Are they proud of their country? Can they stand tall and sing the national anthem with that gleam in their eyes. Kushians are failing to conceptualise and feel in their bones that it's their land and they are the guardians.

"I marvel when I see the Americans sing their anthem. They sing with passion and believe in their country. Slavery has its' legacy and heart-wrenching effects; we are also orchestrating the same system that will affect our next generations."

"The poverty advertisement appear on every channel. Our poor kids paraded with boogies, starving and gasping for air, fed from plastic bag foods."

"Dumbo after that we enjoy the food competitions with people gorging themselves to death and the fat boot camps, its ironic."

"Speaking of overseas Daniel are you going to the embassies how many do we have anyway? Your scheme is just a waste of time. Are you that detached from your people that you need to go on this gallivanting venture? Undercover my foot!! Where did you get this idea from anyway?"

"Abroad, I suppose on TV everything has gone virtual. Daniel, you cannot Skype and tweet but you watch all these international programmes. Some presidents are on tweeter and they campaign online my friend."

"Sit down Dumbo I am serious, I will come back a changed man. I want to tell Kushians the reality, myself."

"After all the United Corporation have put us through."

"Sshh … Daniel."

"No one will hear us I told you it's safe down here in the basement."

"How do you think the financiers will let you go around and work abroad and within. They will take you down this is ridiculous you need your head examined."

"Listen Dumbo, It's because of me you are where you are. You know I am the player and you are a follower, so shut up and listen."

"We have messed up bad and I need to release myself by going; say on this spiritual journey."

"I know the world is in a mess, we who decide have no clue what the ordinary person is going through. Right now a few miles from Kush House they have no electricity and water. We have generators on standby, every place we go everything works."

"Okay, I hear you, Daniel, then why not start by making sure the electricity works everywhere in Kush then go wherever you want to go. You sold a third of our electricity shares to the Malaysians, Daniel."

"We are not different from the rich and famous, we are so stuck-up head to toe in luxury, we have no clue what it feels like to have nothing. We are numb."

"I do not believe the Bible meant Africans to enjoy poverty. It's a Machiavellian intelligence theory. Meekness is about your heart it's not what you have. Rich or poor we can give away something. Time, service, money, education, free lessons. Money is magnified more it's sad"

"It's the transitional stage of being in need, then striving to succeed; the difference is a life lesson learnt."

"That humbling experience is meekness which is the human push to pursuits of the good life which is good health, social, spiritual, financial, physical and sexual."

"Daniel we are not born and bred in riches, where did we get it wrong? Check all these so-called celebrities did they all start in their opulence."

"Watch what you are eating, have your dog with you always and give it what you eat first. Before you go, please make sure that we get enough aid from the Chinese.

"Give me a break Dumbo and get going with your programme. Handouts, aid, do-gooders and United Corporations, I am sick of this game Dumbo."

"Calm down darling." Dumbo patted Daniel on the shoulder.

"Shut up Dumbo! I am not your darling I should get you sanctioned for not calling me, President Daniel Simba." They all laughed as good old friends.

"Kiki is waiting. Dumbo, I heard she has redone her boobies and lips, how is love on the plastic lane." Daniel gave Dumbo the look of love.

"Oh easy tiger, now you touching a plastic nerve; I don't see much of her these days, number two is all real and on the most wished list."

The two presidents chuckled as Dumbo prepared to leave.

"See you Mr President and sleep over your scheme. Are you sure we do not need more intelligence for your security?"

Dumbo was at the door putting his jacket on.

"Goodbye Dumbo; let me work out the plan with my personal adviser."

Gone Fishing

President Simba took some time-out during weekends to visit his ailing father, Kobi at the farm. Daniel invested a lot in making it a dream home and sanctuary for his family. Standing on 100 hectares of land and a small lake, they specialise in horticulture and keep a few farm animals for home use. Entrance to the homestead has beautifully manicured lawns and an array of flowers. The two men walked to their favourite fishing spot; each armed with a tumbler filled with worms and two fishing rods. Both being competitive they could sit for hours just watching intensively to see who catches the first bite.

"Daniel son we are out in the woods, it's time to talk you are never this quiet what is going on, is something bothering you?

Daniel did not expect this question, he did not realise how his manner was so obvious, Maya kept asking and now his father.

"Papa it is nothing to worry about, I know you know me well but it's nothing I cannot fix." Daniel fidgeted with his rod.

"That's it…. you breaking the fishing code of conduct; you do not do that, you now affecting my side keep still young man. Tell me today, I might not live tomorrow what is bugging you, son, you cannot fool me, Dan."

"Papa I carry a heavy load, the whole country on my shoulders. It's becoming too hot to handle."

"Listen Dan Simba I was not born yesterday, and wisdom does come softly. I am not the most obvious person to display emotions and issues of faith. I know that Kingdoms are put up by God and put down, good and bad. The Bible has given us a good example of the legacy of Kings and rulers since the beginning of time. Those that served God continued and those that abandoned him fell, by the way, side."

"You cannot serve God and Mammon, son, choose. The people of Kush need good leaders with wisdom to lead. Son, the hope of Kush, has to base on faith, excellence, wisdom, ethics and virtues. We cannot build our communities out of chaos. Faith values are the foundation of many charities. You cannot lead people without some moral guidelines, which define you. Theories you learn from Universities are not enough to lead people. It's the human in you that people see first.

"Pa I have this dream that keeps hounding me since I moved into Kush House. It's a recurring dream of children crying and asking me for help. It's a very intense dream. I feel drained after each episode."

"Oh, my son it might just be your concerns for Abel and Jude being away from home. Maya is a praying woman she gets them covered spiritually. You need to take it easy and relax more. It might be that you are too stressed."

"How is it with politics and governing the people? We never get to talk about how you are managing. Son, it seems that people are finding life unbearable."

"Papa it's just difficult to explain my circumstances and how I became............

"Who is your daddy?..... Tell me it's a big fish, it's a snapper Yippee." Kobi, Daniels father, interrupted him.....he was so jubilant and always the one who caught first."

Daniel's mind was planning to get even with his Papa. Daniel thought…Uhmm.… just as well he did not reveal his innermost secret of his rise to power.

"Saved by the fish. Pew!" Daniel hissed.

Daniel was happy to keep the sleeping dogs lying. He knew he might go to his grave with the secret tucked in his heart, he had signed an oath. He never had time to ponder over the issues of faith. Life was a roller coaster ride and no time to question and dive the deep end of the soul, seeking the meaning of life. He just thanked each day as it rose and set.

Games of Dominance

The United Corporations meet each year at a secluded place in Alaska. The top brass movers and shakers of the United Corporations take timeout to gather and measure the progress on world governance. They meet in a secret place and rarely is media present. The agenda is about the global economic trends. The year 2011 was a productive year for the United Corporations forecast. The year 2666 is set as the target year for global economic control.

The United Corporation's arms department is the Red Nights. It's the most active subsidiary of the United Corporations. The operations team of Bob, First and Finish, are in charge of African affairs. The main business is the supply of military ammunitions to rebel groups and legitimate governments. The arms trade is the cash cow of the global empire. The principle behind the war video games is fully clear in how the United Corporations' Empire plays a game of chess and monopoly. Red Nights mercenaries provide arms to both rebels and legitimate governments.

Like a video game which they call games of dominance, they watch from a distance. The electronic logistics and tactics board with a world map spread is on an adjustable frame.

Recruiting willing mercenaries was not a problem, the global recession provided many young, educated students and experienced security personnel.

The diversity of cultures provides the Red Nights with a right mix of mercenaries from around the globe. Men and women take up this dangerous and well-paid venture as the world is in recession.

The new stealth hover aircraft technology system enables them to target strategic positions of feuding sides, to get the intended results. Bob, Start and Finish use the tactic board for strategizing the next mission using a simulator similar to the video games in the offices.

Physicists, scientists, doctors and every professional that matters is on the United Corporation payroll. The workers and many world leaders all over the world are oblivious to the real agenda as this group fully exercises its God-given talents to maximum destruction. The rewards are just numbing and hypnotising; this makes the subjects serve the corporation without questioning.

The Kush agenda was a done deal. Getting rid of President Zorro was an easy operation, they did not meet resistance. Kushians were excited about their freedom and independence from colonial rule. The innocence of the electorate and a novice government made it easy for the Red Nights to play their games of dominance.

The victims both rebels and legitimate governments did not know what hit them, left, right and centre. No political analysis could make out what had just happened in Kush as the new government of Daniel Simba took over.

The Red Nights mercenaries moved in place years before the death of Zorro. Money talks and this put many Kushians into unpatriotic positions, a hungry man is a desperate man.

As far as managing their agenda the Empire infiltrated every possible area of influence. The local head chef at Kush House had worked in state house since the colonial era.

Zorro's chief of staff being an innocent man, he allowed the chef to stay to keep the state house functioning. He is a world class chef and caters for all tastes. With the coming inauguration and state House galas, Zorro wanted continuity in Kush house. Mrs Zorro could not object, she is a simple and humble woman. She spent most of her life taking care of her ailing parents as Zorro gallivanted between countries looking for refuge. She had no idea what recipes and cuisine to serve in the state house.

United Corporations appointed a dietician to help the Chef in food preparation. The reward was handsome, quietly he was cooking to instructions. The Chef had no idea the dietician is part of a clandestine activity. It was a gradual process of arsenic poisoning.

A medical personnel was also on hand to give the necessary diagnosis until Zorro's final day. The death of Zorro was a clear sign of the dollar sign, where death becomes insignificant and morals become obsolete. The dollar sign turned brother against brother, father against son, tribe against tribe and a nation against nation.

Farmer's Son

Tom Dumbo is the son of a prosperous black farmer in Kush. Unlike most of his colleagues at boarding school, his father never struggled to pay his fees. The area where their grandfather, Chief Dumbo ruled is within the fertile belt of Kush. Oasis rich soil areas is where most white settlers had annexed. Hard work and good work ethics motivated farmer Dumbo to use the resources he had.

The farm manager got his training from Kush's best Agricultural Institute. With a natural gift and skills, Dumbo farm has prospered. It's now a breadbasket of Kush. The farm uses the old chitemene system of farming by letting the land lay fallow for seven years. The soil rejuvenates and the Dumbos use little pesticides and fertilisers. The Dumbos live comfortably and share their fortune with the community.

Tom was struggling with his schoolwork and some teachers even talked about his short term attention span. His nickname at school was 'Dumb, Dummy' Tom loathed it so much. He was a short stubby boy, quiet and kept to himself. When the schoolmates started taunting him, he would join in the laughter and scurry to the dormitory and cry under the sheets.

The constant picking from his schoolmates was affecting his speech, he would stammer and mumble to say a word.

Tom lost confidence and isolated himself from his schoolmates. Pupils only loved him when his father brought his goodies every month-end. He has a special cupboard made to accommodate his groceries; not heard of at any boarding school.

Little did the father know that Dumbo is paying ransom groceries to avoid beatings from older boys. By the end of the first week, Tom looked at an empty cupboard as the senior boys helped themselves to his food.

When Tom was home, he comes out of his scary shell. His mother always wondered why he is so skinny when he comes back from school and balloons when he is home. She asked a teacher friend, to keep an eye on Tom, only to discover that Tom is under siege.

The Dumbos supported the school with cheap food supplies and gave school fees to poor kids. When the Principal heard about Tom's bullying, he was livid. The chief culprits went to the Principal, he gave them a whipping with a cane until the skin was raw. They could not sit for days and the parents did not say a word. They knew how much Mr Dumbo did to help the poor kids and how their kids had also benefited. For two years, Dumbo did not say a word and suffered in silence.

Tom's father Mr Dumbo came to the school one day and started a club called the mentors club. Senior boys mentored younger boys by seeing to their needs socially and emotionally.

The seniors had to teach young boys about kindness, helping the poor students so everyone can enjoy their days at school.

A trophy was available every year to the best mentor. Though Tom was an average student, he tried in his advanced level subjects and passed with Credits. The Principal thanked Dumbo's mentor for being patient and helping Dumbo to go through his lessons and homework. Dumbo's mentor got the award for the best mentor that year. Dumbo's father wanting not to be outdone, he gave University fees to Dumbo's mentor.

"What can our son be?" Dumbo's father asked.

"He likes telling stories and can talk in detail what has happened and can analyse." Tom's mother interjected

"Journalist," Tom told his parents that he always wanted to be a journalist.

The years of enforced silence at high school and watching TV seeing young journalists badgering interviewees fascinated Tom. He wanted to gain skills to bring out the truth from his interviewees. What makes them tick and make them confess their inner thoughts?

Journalism Tom thought was going to unchain his past and put him on a pedestal.

Tom Dumbo went to study in Russia without delay and started by doing a foundation diploma before gaining his Bachelor's degree.

The nightlife and freedom from bullies got to Dumbo's head and he deferred twice before completing his degree.

As he started to mix and mingle with people of influence in Russia he met Caleb and Daniel at a fund-raising event for journalism students from Kush. United Corporations had seen the potential link with the two cronies and made sure that Dumbo is indoctrinated to the same path. The rest is history.

Kush Geeks

Caleb Biti came a long way to become Personal Adviser to President Daniel Simba. A Harvard graduate who qualified for selection from Mase Mission School to study abroad on a scholarship. Caleb joined Daniel at Harvard and was aware that he is a relation but a cousin many times removed. They never made a big deal about it and just trotted on with their Philosophy, economics and politics degrees.

"Caleb, you can take me out of the woods but can never take the woods out of me, I feel melancholic and homesick my friend." Daniel missed his home cooking.

The sudden change of lifestyle and first world exposure had surely been a jostle socially, emotionally and otherwise but they were managing somehow. Daniel always quizzed his friend Caleb.

"Why do geeks fuss so much about makeup. They use chemicals to bleach their teeth and poison to freshen themselves up. Tweezers to pick hairs from eyebrows and nose. That hideous practice of waxing their hairs." Daniel always challenged the other students but they stuck to their ways.

"Why do men have to be so meticulous about appearance, what about the good old real men, strong and hairy? Men in touch with their compassionate side what is that: Ugh; that's why the world is in a mess no real men to lead."

"I am yet to see the world better for everyone, tell me which century? We need that compassionate side to solve the savagery and brutality man unleash on earth." Caleb was quick to answer Daniel.

Daniel is always at his best in lectures; he is a genius the students know it and professors love him. They were fortunate to create a clique with Professor Small, a well-known Classics professor and international author. No one could understand how these two strange boys; could have won this lonely squinted, sixty-five-year-old man' attention.

Professor Small told the two boys at the end of their studies that their passion and zest made him ask for another teaching extension at the University. Whether it's at the Library, he was with them showing them the tricks of a bookworm. Research journals and, reference books he is there to guide them through, they never let him down. Going home for Professor Small is a scary ordeal, his wife had passed away. His wife did everything for him and now these boys at times visited and fixed a meal to share. His house is within the campus, it is easy to commute on his bicycle.

Professor Small in one of his quips with the boys he says,

"Hey boys you keep my grey matter rich and silky, I might just do another doctorate. Or go with you to Africa I need to reconnect with my roots."

"Easy Professor," Caleb chided Professor Small.

"Allow the young to get our chance first, then the world is your oyster. But Sir that's a search in the dark have you done any research on your lineage."

"Trust me I have, it's a long history and a long flight to my freedom country. We were shipped from the coastal areas in Gambia. I am not sure of my tribe still figuring it out." They all chuckled.

"It is surreal Mr Small, us being here at Harvard and you as our professor. It's humbling how you made it this far. Watching roots was like watching a Holocaust in a different era. The pain is beyond human understanding."

"Humans are fearfully and wonderfully made, we bounce back. Its human resilience and sheer survival that keeps the earth going round. Amid hell on earth, an angel dares to make a difference through personal sacrifice. Universal changes were brought about by humans who were moved, despite the fact they subscribe to some of the slavery ethos."

"Our mothers took care of the plantation master's kids, such bonds cannot be broken. Nursing wet mothers and young women were treated as wenches, used against their will. Amid the hate and loathing, human nature was prevailing. Which is love, compassion, reliance and relationships? There is always one, who dares challenge the status quo and let the people free."

"It's happened in many countries. Here we are to tell the tales. Love has to take precedence, we can only change this world through love."

It was a packed lecture room as professor Small pottered about and fixed the private address system. Every Tuesday, students from different faculties converged to listen to some of his free lectures on Justice. The topic was,

"Rights To The Promised Land."

Caleb was a sensitive man raised by a police officer father with discipline and manners. The two cronies complemented each other and compensated each other's weaknesses. After four years at Harvard, the two became a gem as they excelled to become refined and astute.

Professor Small always reminded his students to question every idea advanced by philosophers.

"For you to say you are an educated person; challenge all fundamental ideals on morality, politics and justice. You cannot allow economic free markets to stifle every core ethic of your existence, question, and challenge. It makes the course exciting and appealing to the mind."

Professor Small would urge his students.

"What is your say on economic fundamentals? We are now living in a capitalist society? It's a dog eats dog, the fundamentals of an equitable market system is slipping away. We need to discuss the issue about the gap between rich and poor."

The two cronies enjoyed the leisure time playing golf here and a spa treatment there, skiing and fine dining. With a P.H.D in Economics and philosophical studies, the future was certain.

Daniel and Caleb wondered where the university got funds for the whole course. When they enquired from the registrar, everything was paid up. The scholarship covered basic studies the extras did not come cheap it baffled the two students.

Abel and Daniel received a call from an agent of the United Corporations for an interview. A limousine was waiting outside to take them to a private gold star hotel in Massachusetts.

Conspiracy Theory

"Welcome gentleman my name is Start my colleague here is Finish. We are representatives of the United Corporations. You are settling in well."

"We have been scouting for talent and watched your journey since you left High school. We have transnational companies around the world and our interests are global. We cause and effect, manipulate and control our business influences all over the world."

"We answer to ourselves and it's not a coincidence that you are here. It's all been in progress and recorded. But listen…We give you credit for your hard work, intelligence and sharp intellect. You have left Harvard with a distinctive stamp of world class education and this has to be put to good use. Listen carefully we have put some money in your Credit Swiss accounts. We have prepared a path for you Daniel Simba; you are to become the next President of Kush."

"What, who, why, how, when?"

Daniel bolted up and his eyes shot out as if about to attack Finish.

It was like an electric jostle from his comfy sofa.

"What about an election process, the electorate do not know me. I never went to war never backed anyone and was still young to understand." Daniel covered his mouth and just slumped back on the sofa.

"Hang on Start...... Is it, or Finish. Who the hell do you think you are, to trounce around and sashay us to this cosy hotel and wham-bam-thank you, ma'am. I am President of Kush. Have you lost your marbles or maybe we are talking to two knuckle airheads on a prank call and we are being framed."

"What do you mean? I planned to work as a lecturer at a university in Kush, not President. I don't have a history attached to the independence struggle, how can I be a President? Liberty Zorro is President, he is a true patriot. He is trying with no help to uplift the people's lives with much difficulty."

"They do not buy his Socialist ideology. Socialism is a starting point for the people of Kush. Capitalism has no place in a liberation struggle. People become bound by the struggles they share, the toils, that's socialism, it's a sentimental ideological process."

"Capitalism has failed and the West knows it. Look at the scandals with the big-time conglomerates. Big banks are a rule unto themselves. Capitalism has created greed with impunity, a few rich and many poor."

"I do not want to lead people for the sake of personal, corporate interests. Daniel excitedly was expressing himself as if he was in a lecture."

"Now listen, Daniel, I am not a patient man," Finish budged in.

"That's where you come in we need to sort out this quagmire and put the people's wishes back on track and not backwards. As long as Zorro rants on about Marxist-Leninist policies and play socialist drums his days are numbered."

"As an organisation we have our interests, we are the guardians of the people of Kush, bona fide benefactors. Someone has to do something than stand and watch Kush just disappear into an abyss. We have seen enough disasters, a stitch in time saves nine."

"Our organisation's background is corporate finance, economics and information technology. Rhetoric cannot bake a pie for every Kushian except for the few rich. That's where we are and where we come in. We are here to help your nation as game changers."

"What do you mean; you are Start and Finish why don't you just finish all this nonsense that you have started; then we can all be happy and head home without much further ado." Daniel was visibly angry.

"Nope, Can't do, you are to stay here at this hotel for the next twelve weeks. We will brief you on every step that we have in-store."

Start looked unconcerned about Daniel's clear confusion, Caleb sat blank eyed and kept staring at the sky as if looking for an answer.

"But" Daniel tried to protest.

"No but; you Caleb, you are in the plan, you will be an adviser to Daniel. You will get your portfolio."

Listen to the News and go to Africa online, be up-to-date. You will get briefings at every stage. Be prepared is the Motto, *comprendo*?"

"We will leave you to digest gentleman; remember your phones and the hotel rooms are bugged. There is nothing we cannot smell, even the whiff from the bathroom. You have no choice."

"Hey.....What sick joke is this, you cannot force us to do this." Daniel followed them to the door threateningly.

"You two have been at our disposal and we can dispose of you and no one will miss you. Mark my words." Start and Finish slammed the door on their way out.

When Start and Finish left abruptly, the two cronies sat in silence.

"Hey, Daniel is this for real?"

"Sshh, let's get some sleep and brew this over in the morning. Look at these crisp white Egyptian cotton linen sheets, this is the life. I am taking my stuff to my room in a minute; just as well it's a presidential suite."

"Oh, I need a drink what the hell is going on." Caleb struggled to his feet.

"The decanter is over there it has some sherry, but Caleb, you do not drink" Daniel was nodding his head, annoyed by Caleb's fidgeting.

"I do now my head is spinning can I call my mum" Caleb appeared like he was in a dream.

Daniel walked towards Caleb, scratching his head.

"Stupid you cannot, she is in the rural areas there are no phones. Calm down Caleb"

"Think about it, they like us these international think tanks. We promoted their line of thinking. It does fit in with the One-World Vision, why do you fear. We shall do exactly what we have debated and reasoned for the last four years. It's not been in vain Caleb; Wow, it is cool. From Harvard to Kush house and the blueprint we have it."

"The President of Kush. Oh wow! Marry, a beautiful wife, maybe they will choose for me. Hell no! It has to be someone I love from the heart, not from the mind." Daniel tried to calm Caleb's obvious nervousness.

"You are an intelligent man Daniel; for what it's worth, you will manage to deal with this. Your country needs you, Daniel."

"No, no. Our country needs us, Caleb. It's weird like déjà vu, looking back how we could not see and tell that everything was just going so smooth and easy for us."

"Our classmates from High school have degrees without any hope of getting a job, last heard that Faro had gone berserk after University. He is now taking weed. He could not cope with the clerical job after gaining a Degree in Accountancy. That's life and how the cookie crumbles Caleb."

"Caleb it's time to use our intellectual minds and human resources to build the economy. We need mentors to become the bedrock and inspire the young minds to go ahead with research and development."

"Talk is cheap Dan, Kushians feel deterred by economic conditions which are not indigenous to serve us. Another problem is looking at someone's tribe and party affiliations before qualifications. That's the curse of the African tribe."

"We are at the mercy of the translational companies and they employ their choices, expatriates from abroad."

"Daniel, my Uncle used to say. Son, my office is the one next to the toilet the Human resources department."

"Uncle said that his office dealt with the locals, workers unions, and wages; away from the big cahoots offices which are plush and polished."

"At Headquarters one sees the big guys that make things happen. The successful blacks have to tour the line. They do not want their offices muddied with dirty overalls from miners and non-office stuff. Uncle was the dartboard for every human resource crisis. It's our people that are the majority wage earners.

The international press always thinks it's us giving our people a bad ride yet it's from near, far and wide. My uncle John died a frustrated man because he had to know where his loyalty lies; with the company or the poor workers. When uncle held meetings to resolve pay disputes, he knew the final decision lay with the House always winning."

"If you understand my saying. Uncle came from a humble family, with work ethics 'If you do not work you shall not eat. He would always tell us."

"The strain of trying to solve the insolvable was overwhelming for Uncle. He collapsed on his swivel chair at night; moonlighting. He was discovered in the morning with his computer on, trying to finish his redundancy proposal plan which he opposed."

"Caleb what can we do with a problem like Africa. Here we are my friend, delving into the unknown with our eyes open, our minds seared. Do we have a choice? Is this United Corporations legit or just a front to use us, abuse us and throw us away? It's a game of dominance. I do not remember Kush ever getting a fair deal.

"To be or not to be is the dilemma" Daniel quipped.

****

Start and Finish were meticulous in their project and did not mince their words. If they said, jump Daniel and Caleb jumped.

They had to go through portfolios with comprehensive information. The two interns discovered the greatness of Kush better than at school in Kush.

Caleb and Daniel developed a flare for details an improvement in their fashion sense a jacket and tie with matching handkerchiefs and cufflinks. In the hotels, it was oysters, crabs and other culinary adventures. Caleb was not complaining, moving from hotel to hotel.

Daniel still talked about the ghetto in him and how he missed his home cooking. Polenta with relish and vegetables. He struggled to adjust his palette to all these different dishes. Daniel found some dishes palatable, it was the fine dining that he detested.

Caleb awakened his thoughts when he said.

"Daniel, why do we have to change our diet to serve our own people? Are we just phoneys what else are we to change, the way we talk, laugh, and dress? We do not need to change our ways to communicate with our people."

Caleb and Daniel had no control over their daily life. They reported to Start and Finish daily, by logging their itinerary.

With a high-spec laptop, it was the masses of information and briefings that kept them engrossed in their next adventure.

After three years in the United States, Daniel and Caleb flew to Russia in business class.

First and Finish planned a quick study in International Law, Business Finance and the Russian revolution. The United Corporation slowly introduced the two cronies to the right contacts in Kush.

Tom Dumbo a Kushian was also doing a journalism degree in Russia. Brief newspaper articles especially the Financial Zone gave positive reviews about the new breed of politicians to get national coverage in Kush.

The local newspapers covered the emerging philanthropists and successful students. Daniel and Caleb became national treasures as they advanced a different approach to Zorro's socialist ideology. They gave funds for scholarships to University faculties.

They looked for intellectuals to spread their goodwill to the rest of the population. Kushians slowly welcomed their lost and found heroes from Harvard and now found in Russia.

The country needed Daniel and Caleb's skills and Zorro was the one heard always telling the country about his boys. He was a well liked President.

"Let's show the world that we are capable of doing anything, we set our mind on."

Zorro liked repeating Martin Luther King quote,

"We should not be judged by the colour of our skin but the content of our character."

Zorro asked Daniel and Caleb privately if they wanted to take part in government.

Daniel knew that he had to keep clear until orders come from United Corporations. Daniel and Caleb were willing to be consultants and offer their services free while they set up their own enterprise. Zorro felt indebted to the two cronies as they advised on many issues which the cabinet had no expertise.

Kush Defence Ministry received aircraft's and ammunition from overseas contacts. The police budget received a vehicle fleet to increase more security for the ministers. United Corporations did not waste time and were also available to give training and intelligence. Daniel and Caleb had contacts and this helped to negotiate deals and private intelligence training for security staff.

The news blast read "**President Liberty Zorro has died,**" Shocked Daniel looked at Caleb and said

"It's time."

The army and the police had sophisticated weapons to deal with any riots after the sudden death of father Zorro the President of Kush. It was thanks to Daniel and Caleb's foresight. The two cronies helped Zorro to buy military equipment and artillery from Alaska. Kushians struggled with the sudden news of Zorro's death. United Corporation wanted stability and advised Kushians to give respect to a man of the soil than cause chaos.

The masses were hoping that there might be a chance to see if Zorro's plans to nationalise the mines was happening. United Corporations took an interest in this small country called Kush. Kushians wondered why.

A transitional government was now in place and Tino Dupo, Zorro's Vice President, was to takeover until the next elections. Daniel's rise to power was not a surprise; he was eloquent and promised the people change.

The technocrats, university students and intellectuals identified with him. The rural folks knew that he grew up in the village. Daniel, a well-educated man, was their choice. Kushians believed he could pull Kush from the dump of despair and bring it into the 21st century. A well connected and respected leader, Daniel was the only choice presented in the media. The attention from the international community was overwhelming.

In the immediate the people saw shifting and changes in the size of cabinet departments. Government reshuffling, people thought as they marvelled at Daniel's rise from somewhere to Kush house.

Sergeant Major's Son

Caleb is a police officer's son and brought up with discipline, in an extreme hygienic environment. His father is the only black officer promoted to Sergeant Major. Caleb is an only child, his mother suffered from multiple miscarriages and gave up.

Women in the police camp take part in baking, knitting, embroidery and cooking competitions. The white police officer's wives supervise all the club activities. Every year the Police camp hosted crafts and athletic events for the families.

There is not a dull moment in the Police camp as most evenings officers meet at the local club to drink and chat about life. The environment caters for families and many officers come with their kids. The club chef was a busy man every Wednesday and weekends as families booked dinners. A pleasant atmosphere and rarely could one see an officer drunk. Officers knew they had to be on their best behaviour. Otherwise, it affected their promotion.

The structures allowed support systems and young cadets always copied their seniors.

Despite the disparities caused by colonial rule, the camp thrived, with many officers settling into married life, children and good education for their families.

The cadets knew that if they wed, the whole community is there to support and encourage them.

During the colonial era, a few blacks occupied positions of authority. In the Police force, the highest rank a black officer could attain was Sergeant Major. Caleb's father Mr Biti was the Sergeant Major, a rank lower than Major. The Chief Police Commissioner held house inspections every half year. They went around inspecting each house checking cleanliness and hygiene. The Police Commissioner was a control freak he detested dirt. One of his notorious tasks was running house inspection more than any other province in Kush. The Province earned a national status as the best-kept police camp in Kush. He always found an excuse to be on the back of his black officers.

The inspections were targeted at black families down to their lowest rank constables. The top hierarchy of the force; the white officer's families hired black nannies and house workers to clean for them. White officers' houses were not inspected. Their quarters were a section away from the black officers'. White folks had more bedrooms and bigger yards and outbuildings even those with small families.

The black families made do with standard houses with minimal space. Caleb's family was the only black family in the white quarters because he was promoted to Sergeant Major.

The separation did affect Caleb as he could not mix much with his own black friends. They just thought of his family as different from them, even though they were a quiet black family who had been promoted.

Caleb learnt to be smart and particular about hygiene issues. His father being part of the administration team he was also in the inspection delegation.

The Chief Commissioner was a man called Kruger he was ruthless and no nonsense man. He expected his camp to be up to scratch no flies or mosquitoes in the houses. Gardens cut, spruced ridges and flowers blooming. Caleb's father sought extra help as he was a senior officer. Prisoners in police cells; who were not risky came to help do the garden. Caleb could not hold a spade he was still a young boy.

Caleb and his mum started cleaning the house a week before the inspection day. The Bitis scrubbed the house from top to bottom. Being an only child Caleb had to learn fast, he did not want his mum to work by herself. Legends boots worn by police officers were polished until one could see a reflection. Caleb spat, spat and polished until the shoes shined. The window frames and water taps were made of bronze. Caleb's mum bought some bronze polish to apply and shine. Windows and floors were cleaned to sparkle and shine like spilt water.

This was a time of bringing out the doilies and best sofa covers made with cross stitch and motifs. Women who can do flower arranging showed their skill on this day of reckoning the inspection day. A day dreaded by black police officer's wives. Each household tried to be creative to decorate and plant flowers in their gardens.

It so happened in one house as the inspection team went into the apartment of a junior Police officer called Pori. A big cockroach went thud on the Commissioner's hat right in the middle of the kitchen. It had suffocated from an aerosol sprayed the night before. The cockroach hung precariously and gave up the ghost.

The code of practice is to spray the whole house with aerosol. Officer's wives usually sit outside for half the day until all the flies, ants and cockroaches give up the ghost.

The Commissioner left the house in a huff; he was visibly angry. The junior officer knew what was coming; a failed report and another inspection two days later. Every police camp dweller hated a failed report, it meant rework and stares from the neighbours. It was more work because of a stubborn cockroach which mistimed its time of death, and the officer possibly getting a demotion.

"Cleanliness is next to Godliness." Caleb's father told his son

"Show me the verse, Papa," Caleb asked his father.

"An ordinary man can also interpret the scriptures. Preachers are still sermonising and personalising scriptures since 2000 years ago, son. Preachers have amassed empires because of their subtle manipulation of the good book."

"How insincere that you can own a private jet by shouting what God has already commanded. It's not a blessing but a blunder."

"How do we live with this mindset, when we take money from the poor and come driving in Bentleys, Mercedes-Benz and Porsches its sick." Biti could be cynical about many things in life.

Caleb could not wait to go to boarding school. His father realised that with the regime of inspections and camp life, Caleb's education could suffer. Mr Biti was on patrol for months in rural lands and missed helping his son.

From twelve years, Caleb went to a boys only boarding school. His mother asked her young cousin, to come and keep her company when Caleb's father was on patrol.

Caleb worked hard from the start, he was a bright and intelligent boy getting A grades in most of his subjects. Caleb had no inkling for girls, he was content being a bookworm. As an only child, Caleb enjoyed his own company and spent his time hidden in books or the school library. An insatiable boy as far as books were concerned.

This solitude did not go unnoticed by the school boarding master, father Jack. He started expressing this boy's genius qualities to the school board.

He asked for permission to work with the young boy. Father Jack wanted to check and see why he distanced himself from other boys.

Caleb was happy to go and see Father Jack's bookshelf. The Library was stocked with a variety of books. From sociology, economics, philosophy, astronomy and science. The books were better than the school's library.

"You can come any time Caleb even Sunday afternoons when others are at sports. I will get your exemption pass, do not worry son."

That was the beginning of Caleb's pains. He did not know what it was the priest wanted him to do. He could not understand and had never seen or been told about men doing such things. Father Jack told Caleb it was just a boy's game. He asked Caleb not to talk or share with anyone lest they see him as a sissy.

His father was always his confidante and Caleb never failed to tell him stories about what the other boys did at school. The night escapes to the girl's mission school a mile away and what they did with the girls. He decided to tell his dad. In turn, his Papa sat him down and chatted about girls. Mr Biti talked about puberty and any questions Caleb wanted to know.

His love for books had not yet taken him to such discoveries. Even Chinua Achebe 'Things fall apart', Cry the beloved country, Macbeth, and his favourite Grisham. They were not direct about boy and girl issues. The bible always said,

"*And the men knew the woman and bore a child.*"

The best girl he knew was his mother and she was Queen Bee and his dad always told Caleb. This new concept of association with an adult man was just too bizarre for Caleb. At the farm, the cousins were curious about chickens and farm animals doing the doodah.

He asked his father in a letter, whether a priest could do such a thing. When the letter got home, it was too late. The priest turned into a raging maniac and bit and violated Caleb when he said,

"No!! I will not come again to your house."

His father did not waste time he arrived at the school brandishing a gun asking for father Jack. He was roughed up by the school boarding master and father Jack was put in safe custody to avoid bloodshed. No one had seen this coming it was more like a tsunami.

"The full force of the law will be upon this school I guarantee you that." Biti screamed and hollered.

Mr Gozo the whip mongering Principal managed to put the situation under control. Mr Gozo was a law unto himself and could not be fuzzed by anyone. The mission school is listed as one of the top five in Kush.

It churned out many bright pupils now scattered abroad. Mr Gozo knew well that one false move on his part. It could mean a disaster that could destroy his reputation, his mission school plus the hundreds of children.

At the back of his mind, he knew that Kush was a beggar. It could not choose, so the sponsors from overseas had the last say. A careful and well thought out strategy was what Gozo carefully planned. He wanted to make sure that he is in control of the situation.

Father Jack could easily go to another vicarage or mission school. The church ran many schools scattered in the country.

Father Jack had developed a reputation without a resume to go with it. He never stayed in mission schools for more than two years. The community knew that father Jack had an itching bottom because he did not settle in one place.

Caleb's father was already helping by taking his son out of the school. Gozo thought one problem down. He knew that he had to quickly find another place for Caleb a bright and brilliant treasure at the school.

"I will be back…..This is not the last you hear from me. Gozo you will pay the full force of the law. I will hound you, take my word, I mean it."

Biti was furious and moving up and down like a raging bull about to charge

Caleb's father did not want to talk he was so angry he could only stomp the floor.

With his son safely in the police truck, school trunk and books were in the back. Mr Biti drove like a blazing maniac leaving a whirlpool of dust like a pending hurricane.

Undercover Meeting

"Mr President the team is here. Remember to use alpha codes we need to get it right." Caleb was meticulous in his execution of tasks and time conscious.

"Caleb, have you done the research on internal audit systems? I prefer the internal audit route because it takes me through the systems. Departments can relax when they realise we are not there to take their jobs."

"The audit team will look at how Ministries can accomplish their objectives."

"This can be achieved by bringing a systematic, disciplined approach. A system able to evaluate, processes too.

"Sure Mr President, Internal auditing, acts more as a catalyst to improve an organisation's governance. It includes risk management and management controls. It does provide insight and recommendations based on analyses and assessments of data, business activities. We need government ministries to commit to ethics, best practice integrity and accountability for a change."

Caleb showed the president the flow chart of the audit operations.

"Caleb internal auditing provides value to governing bodies and top management. It is an objective source of independent advice."

"We should not shy away from such management tools. External auditing is broad and entails us justifying using the well-known companies like Earnest and Young. I do not want the government wing of the Comptroller General involved, this is my audit. I will do it my way."

"Caleb make sure you select men to be in the team. I want to be the Audit Overseer Manager, this way I can speak to staff and let the professionals carry on with the tasks."

"Why do you want men only on the audit team?" Caleb looked quizzically at Daniel.

"Women can easily pick a scent, I do not want any competition. Women are good at smelling a rat they can sniff each other out. If I have to dress as a woman and be the Mrs Black Doubtfire. Guys will leave me alone to get on with my stuff, age is my score, no one will pass a second look."

"Ohm, well that should work. I knew you could come up with a brilliant idea, a *modus operandi*. Operation Undercover; good luck Mr President." Caleb patted Daniel on the shoulder.

"Not yet, the worst is yet to come. Caleb was now putting on his jacket. Let's go in and get the ball rolling." Daniel scurried after Caleb.

Caleb announced the president's arrival in the Octagon office. This was an unusual meeting it was under closed doors and security on alert to prevent unwelcome guests.

****

"Calling the meeting to order; I will make this brief and to the point. You are the only personnel that is privy to this information and, therefore, top secret. This operation is an undercover assignment. An officer whom you do not know of yet will go undercover. She will follow internal auditors as they do brief audits on selected ministries and a few embassies? Your assignment is to provide security and backup. Caleb will provide the itinerary details as soon as possible. Caleb will prepare a draught plan to work with. The assigned personnel is code Zee and it's she."

"She will be the overseer manager of the internal audit team. Why do we need to keep a tab on her you might ask? It is because I, the President need her feedback, so I can truthfully address the nation before the end of the year. You see now why we need to protect her, she is a gem."

"Caleb is going to work with her side by side. I am happy that Caleb knows about Auditing, Finance and many government operations."

"That's why he is my adviser." Daniel stood and the rest of the team followed.

The team just nodded their heads and were always petrified when called to do any covert operations for the President. They were trained by an intelligence company from abroad. Kushians questioned the mysterious death of many members of the opposition.

This secrecy silenced the electorate and the masses had to gullibly accept the new unknown Daniel Simba to be their President.

In Kush, rumours were circulating that President Zorro was poisoned and forensic tests were not done. The United Corporations announced in the media that the country needs stability. Therefore, alarm bells were no help. Daniel diligently took on his role with impunity. The smart team was swift and skilful, as long as the President made sure they get paid in time, loyalty was not a problem. They knew which side their bread is buttered.

Caleb and Daniel went down to the basement for a further review of the programme. The basement was designed for emergencies like coups and chemical warfare. It is a safe haven; with an escape route to the Falcon hotel. President Daniel Simba has access to the keys as part of his package. The Falcon presidential suite is available three hundred and sixty-five days a year to the president.

Daniel surprised many friends he never liked a drink he always drank water. Caleb since Harvard he had a sip here and a sip there. Today he needed one. Caleb, knew he had started something that could have devastating effects on Daniel's presidency, and the nation.

Caleb's flare for detail and his unusual savvy upkeep was going to come in handy. His upbringing in a police camp had given him a touch for things classy.

"Come tie my hair, bring me my powder and manicure set" Caleb's mum would call out.

His mother relied on him to pull the zip-up and take stockings from the drawer. He learnt to apply nail vanish and false eyelashes. Caleb's mother kept head mannequins with different wigs for each occasion.

Mrs Biti was expected to keep up appearances at the local officer's gala. Many times she went with her husband to the senior police officer's functions. Caleb became an expert on fashion combinations and makeup. He always set quietly in a corner watching his parents dance. Unfortunately, he had to go to the events and take note of any fashion highlights to make his dear mama stand out.

Many times the Bitis practised ballroom dancing and the only free companion in the daytime at home was her son Caleb. Mrs Biti was in charge of helping the policewomen to cook and Caleb became the drink connoisseur and food taster.

He learnt fast and furiously as many kids could not place him when boys did rough play in the playgrounds. They would call him salad at school because of his unusual dietary needs.

Realising what he had started Caleb pinched himself many times. He had to remind himself that he was responsible for such risky adventure never done by any President.

"Daniel I will be with you throughout. No one will know it's you. I will deal with your makeover. I will make sure it's done in a proper way and not sweaty and greasy under the wigs."

"Do not make a pass at me Caleb you know how handsome I am, and can easily pass for my sister."

"Yeh, Yeh, hear, hear I will take care of that goatee." Caleb was inspecting Daniel.

The president always wondered why Caleb never married. He had not seen him take an interest in women.

President Simba thought Caleb was always perfectly dressed. He had a tendency to be excessively compulsive with hygiene issues. Staff rumoured that he wiped his chair before he sat. Caleb scrubbed his hands every time he used the bathroom.

"Ohm, I have a draft plan for you to look at. I have sent the memos of our pending visits Daniel. We can safely say this exercise is a feasibility study; to survey how we are coping with management information systems."

"Let them know this is an Indigenous sponsored programme, so that some smart Alec will not raise eyebrows. They will snoop and start asking about Hansard report or statutory instrument this or that."

"Do not worry Daniel, Josh Green will have a brilliant audit team to cover your back."

"Caleb I will skin you alive if they ever find out; I dressed in some women's clothes. Do you know how taboo this is? I cannot even begin to think about me in a dress. Caleb this is absurd and an African President for that matter it is suicide by acid. The western media will create a frenzy over this Caleb."

"I can become the laughing stock of the whole world. I have not had time to even think about the disguise you know. I am a fashion disaster but for this adventure; Harrods here I come."

"Get me the finest dresses Caleb. Make sure they are elegant and cover my ugly legs."

"Daniel, you are incorrigible, can you walk with high heels? Who used to laugh at the Nicky, picky and plucking grooming geeks at Harvard? Look who is Mrs Doubt on fire now?"

"But man do put on dresses all the time. Our Nigerian and Ghanaian brothers wear long dashiki gowns same as the women. It's very lovely African attire indeed. They do look like half dresses over matching trousers?"

Daniel was hysterical gasping for air as he slumped in his swivel chair.

"It will work and this is the most excited I have been since our Harvard years it's like seeking truth again without any external influences."

"But Daniel you are in deception trying to get to some understanding. With all the security details and disguises; come on man."

"There are guys around you who want a chance at the helm and it's becoming dirty out there trust me."

"I do not know whom to trust anymore." Daniel agreed with Caleb.

"Just heard from intelligence guys, what happened in the north province? Who gave orders to massacre those people poor in a village who have nothing? I am smarter than that Caleb."

"I just do not wily, nilly give orders to exterminate a village. Why? To give me a bad name I suppose?"

"That is why Daniel you have to go undercover you are bound to hear some nasty stuff about who is who in the game. You can never trust anyone in politics that is why it's called a dirty game. It could even be the Red Nights mercenaries playing their dominance games with Kush. Remember that area has the best minerals."

"This is the beginning of the end of my life Caleb but I am determined. I took Maya off guard and just told her it's a working holiday assignment. She is all bought out and ready for their holiday. So are you ready Caleb for an adventure of our lifetime, from a small Village to Harvard to Kush house then undercover."

"Daniel despite the United Corporations' strings that are tied to you. I do admire your resolve. You have accepted to think outside the box to explore and see the country's goings on for yourself. It is so easy to be complacent and relax in the luxury and opulence.

We have become insensitive, indifferent and pitiful to those that are poor and it's happening everywhere. Go and see the evil behind the country's veil."

"I now know that money is the root of all evil. Mind-set, discipline and a sense of purpose are a disciplined process. We are busy preaching tribalism and divisive ranting that do not bring the people together."

"Kushians want to experience a United Nation but we are busy pleasing the master. We need more inspirational leaders from within to inspire our children. The rappers, unfortunately, preach gangster and cursing our people. Insulting our women."

"Our kids are the champions of swearing why? We are also champions of bottom wiggling. Daniel, I want our kids to be champions of science and technology."

"They must unravel the mysteries of this universe, but alas. Creativity which does not need brains and too much thought is what our kids have platform."

"All these traits and actions are raising a generation no longer sensitive to shame or dignity. It is now cool to be dysfunctional. Ask any of our kids which black person they admire. Nine times out of ten it is a rapper. Look at the pomp and ceremony when they are on stage. It's not about enlightenment but self-distraction, drugs, self-praise and bottom wiggling."

"But in all this chaos, the kids need to be heard. This rap music has messages of reality too, but is it the only way to present ourselves to the next generation? It's not that everyone can be refined, we need to be leaders who can show wisdom and nation building."

"God is a Creator and we are the created beings we have creative gifts. Yes, we have different gifts but nothing good can come out of chaos."

"We need an organised society so that each individual can reveal their creative gifts."

The First Lady

When Maya walks into a room, everyone takes notice she has an aura that catches attention. A beautiful, elegant woman and she knew it. Maya is slender and has a well-toned body, unlike many of her age and persuasion. At 35 years, she visits the gym and jogs three times a week. An ardent reader with an MSc in Finance under her belt. Maya, a high-profile executive with one of the local Merchant banks, handling the investment division. A pro tennis player and keen swimmer.

Daniel vowed not to toe the line and find a woman of his own choice. Everywhere he went, whether it's a gala or cricket match she was there. On one of the many dinner parties hosted by Zorro, Maya sat next to Daniel and they hit it off like a house on fire. At the back of his mind, he still wondered whether Start and Finish were involved in placing Maya at the right time and place.

That was the beginning of the rest of their relationship. Daniel tried to piece things together to track if Start and Finish were involved. He failed to solve the puzzle. Maya looked innocent, unpretentious and unaffected around Daniel. Daniel assigned his own private investigator to check Maya's background and nothing was out of sorts. Maya earned her way to University with her working class parents behind her success.

Just an ordinary Kush family with a daughter who has her head firmly screwed on and looks to compliment.

The wedding was beyond a dream, Maya looked stunning and President Liberty Zorro gave his blessings. He wanted other technocrats to follow Daniel's example of hard work by building a career, helping parents and finding a wife to settle down. When Maya thought of something, she made sure she saw it through. No one could stand in her way.

Due to the ever present pressing issues in the country, Daniel was a busy President. Maya took time off to go out to the farm to have solitude and invaluable quiet space to recharge her batteries. She always made it known to Daniel that her quiet moments are sacred. Daniel knew he had married the right woman who could stand being alone. A woman who could manage without being clingy and in his face demanding this and that. It gave Daniel space to look at life and conceptualise the junk in the trunks of his country.

At their wedding, President Zorro decided to be a story teller .....

"Once upon a time, there are two young university graduates; one from Kush and one Jewish, given £10000 to start a business. The Kush entrepreneur rents an office gets some cousins, nephews and a secretary to do import and export in African jewellery.

He buys a Porsche on company credit card and starts gallivanting and visiting hotels with Mr, Miss, Mrs and Ms, entertaining till the break of dawn on a business tag. The young man uses bank overdrafts to meet his debts.

The relatives become disgruntled. The bank calls in the loans and he is put into liquidation. He has not filed company returns to the registrar of companies, he has no time to do the accounts."

"The Jewish boy rents out the flat goes to buy a piece of land dresses in khaki shorts and shirts, gets a part-time job for upkeep. He asks mum and dad to allow him to put up while he sees to his plantation. He buys seeds gets seasonal workers to plant and maintain the project. The young man can not afford a girlfriend. He is stuck in hobbies like reading, fishing, golf and white water rafting to keep his mind off women."

"After 5 years the harvest came and the timber did not disappoint he gets a healthy return on his investment and a possible yearly harvest after that. He has profits and declares dividends and goes for a holiday finds a wife and has money ever after."

President Zorro reminded his people:

"Through hard grafting and focus our reward is guaranteed. In the process, wisdom will come softly to enable us to maintain the wealth and growth.

Short-term aggrandisement is a disease that Kushians have to fight as a people."

"Parents think of your children's future; write down their goals. Put pen to paper and list your goals, meditate on these goals for your children."

"Stop shouting, hollering and venting frustration at your kids. Talk, please learn to talk so that, civilisation can come."

"If we talk and bicker and no one is listening. I tell you it is a recipe for disaster. Let's listen to each other than talking over each other."

"From home to school to the office to the whole nation, learn to listen more." Zorro always urged his country.

"God gave us one mouth and two ears, listen more than talk. Let's change our perspective on life, be a people that are happy for one another."

"Push each other up not down he said. Ph.D. should not be a (Pull Him Down) qualification, offered at any place of knowledge in the country. It should be a Push Him Up; a PHU."

"If we can just be a people known to be happy and driven, looking out for one another no matter our standing then civilisation is realised."

"A country's democracy should be measured by how we treat our own vulnerable people. Especially the poor, the orphan, children, the widow and the needy."

"Our children are a spectacle the whole world, in the most uncomfortable way. With boogies and flies, emaciated with kwashiorkor it's the saddest showcase I have ever seen. It seals the state of Kush seeing little kids like that."

"We need to step up and not wait for people to fly over and take care. We are all abrogating our responsibilities. Where is the Kushian spirit _it takes a village to raise a child?"

"Despite our struggles to gain independence, if we say today let's close our borders. We tell everyone to look out for the poor and needy we can all do it; then a culture is enriched. Let's pray that our vulnerable young people are not drawn into getting guns from mercenaries."

"Remove this endemic Kushian reliance on the gospel fear of the unknown and mistrust. It's counter productive and barbaric."

"That is why we cannot expect remorse if it's any loss of human life in Kush. Whether caused by others or ourselves because we do not respect ourselves." Zorro was King Kush.

****

As President Daniel Simba took the reins of power, the country was now gearing towards a new social order. The country geared towards monopolies running wild. The general electorate went along with sentiments of the elite they trusted their professional students.

"Change we need, change we can," They shouted in unison.

The naked kids in the rural areas, the schoolkids at the assembly, the father in a factory, workers in underground mines. In the office, they shouted for Change. From socialism to capitalism the Kush nation battled to channel its economy to recovery. In Kush, it was protectionism versus open markets. Forecasters said that it needs a good juggler from the circus to steer this Kush ship-to-shore.

Kushians want to work hard and make Kush a proud and beautiful country. The reality for many was that it is a long walk to freedom. Someone was holding them back it was more like hitting a wall especially with issues that directly benefit the local people.

Daniel's nomination for the presidency was not contested he appeared from nowhere. Kush wanted stability and he was the best available candidate after Zorro's death. The transition to power was smooth amid the great expectations. His credentials, a Harvard degree, his stint in Russia and a philanthropist. It gave him a resume that Kushians are willing to accept. The icing on the cake was his beautiful and elegant wife, Maya at his side. Daniel chose his cabinet with Dumbo as deputy and Caleb his adviser. Daniel felt at ease to play this political game. With Maya on his side and the United Corporation confidence, Daniel felt invincible.

As President Simba was struggling with a heavily indebted economy, Kushians were anxiously waiting for change.

Start and Finish kept quiet for a while and Daniel came to realise there is a substitute in their midst. The United Corporations come in many faces, all colours, religions, businesses they were astute and sharp.

In one of Daniel's private talks with Caleb, they worked it out that it was still business as usual with the United Corporations. A religious group well set up in the country was heavily involved in politics. At one of their secret meetings in a private country club right in Kush farming area, Daniel met the brethren.

The meetings are conducted in secret and this association of men has no colour barrier. Their call is to self-realise and reach the highest potential.

****

"Mr President the programme is ready and the itinerary is set, but it needs your perusal."

Caleb was in the basement office the most private area of Kush house. The poor network made it impossible to receive communication, which is why Daniel preferred it for his secret meetings.

"How many embassies are we able to cover?" Daniel asked Caleb.

"One in Europe, Middle East and Africa, it is easier with the embassies they are small offices.

"Caleb this is it." United Corporations will not be able to suss us out. I have access to the presidential suite and the smart team always swipe it before I go every time.

I need to use the secret emergency passage for this operation. It leads straight to the suite. I think no one at the hotel will know my movements as I change disguise. You being there its double the security."

"With outlying areas I will be able to touch base and visit the villages and chat with our stronghold the rural electorate. If the internal audit manager is ready, then let's start. As you said, it's more about management information systems. We also need to look at compliance and improvements. Yes, let's get the ball rolling." Daniel was eager to finish what he had started.

"I am ever ready Sir."

"You know something Caleb the computer systems are just changing every day. From storage systems, the size of Kush house or bigger to tiny memory chips on my small finger. Incredible my friend…. but anyway we know our mission is impossible. The makeover, any briefing on that?" Daniel was surely ready and set to go.

"Your clothes Mrs Soti are tailor-made to suit and the wigs are easy to glue on, so there is no chance of accidents. With a bald head like yours and clean-shaven it is a hairdresser's dream makeover. I did order court shoes size 10 they are easier to walk in. You do not have to worry about having modelling lessons."

"Do not make it awkward Caleb." Daniel protested.

"I had to order from America I could not find a woman's size ten at Harrods in London. Hold on Madam, your brazier will have chicken fillets for boobs to give, you know what I mean. The oomph and va, va vroom."

Caleb laughed hard as he gestured the actions as a woman pushing the bosom. Well, they are padded to give you some boobs Mr President."

"Goodness gracious me, chicken what?" The two cronies bellowed with laughter amid tears and stomach cramps.

"Am I going to get an Oscar for this?"

"No; you will get best female actress."

"Oh my word, I honestly forgot that I need boobs, wow you got that sorted already. Chicken fillets are they raw Caleb? Please do not make it an extreme makeover. This is bizarre never realised how complex a female species is?"

"You cannot pull this off without boobs my friend. They will sit perfectly on you, a C cup size that is lemon size not too much attention from the guys feel it, its plastic" Caleb was almost crushing the small fillets.

Daniel lost his composure and belted a laugh, he had never done for years. He gasped for air \holding on to the chair.

"Caleb you see how we missed harmless adventures. I think this is a midlife crisis or misplaced identity.

We cooped up in Harvard studying like bookworms, this is a midlife crisis, my friend. We are trying to recreate lost youth adventures."

"Remember how we fervently tried to refuse what this United Corporation brought to us. We could have been doing something else freely my friend, without looking over our shoulders. We never had a chance to ensemble women on our meagre student wages. We lost too much youth time, my friend."

"It's going to be the most hilarious adventure ever undertaken by a President. The sad thing is no one will know where you have been."

"Daniel do you ever take a moment to think about a possible foul-up and potential spill."

"Absolutely, I hope the audit team will be as good as they are said to be." Caleb wanted to see if Daniel had thought things through.

"It's the audit team that I have to catch up with. That is why we will keep a distance, let them do the audits and I be an overseer. It will work. I have the liberty to be anywhere I want to be. I can come home if there is an emergency."

****

The first meeting of the audit team was at the Falcon, a prestigious 5-star hotel in Edom, the capital city of Kush. Daniel used the shuttle from the basement to the hotel without any hiccups for the first time. With no one in site, Daniel pressed the button in the shuttle.

The smooth and noiseless transport was just like in Star Trek he thought.

"Boldly going where no man has gone before," Daniel imagined the popular TV series.

The entry door was just next to the President's bedroom suite in a study room. The secret door opens as a bookshelf discreetly. Few people knew about this passage. Daniel felt like an undercover sleuth just like in the movies, as he walked into his presidential suite. The arrangement was that Caleb goes by car so he can check that security is on spec.

"Sit still Daniel, you have to get this right just a bit of glue to fix the wig; do not be impatient with me." With much fluffing and cajoling, Mrs Soti emerged.

"Hey who is this woman?" Daniel looked, in the mirror. He put his hands on the hips and swayed from side to side without rhythm.

"Daniel you look amazing, you are indeed, Sara's twin sister." Caleb could not hold his surprise.

Daniel did look like his sister Sara. Caleb started giggling when Daniel tried to readjust his bra. It just looked awkward and he squealed with laughter.

"I am free" Daniel pretended to be Humphreys on; '*Are you being served*' a British comedy programme.

"You cannot be Humphreys he is a guy but Mrs Slocomb." Caleb corrected Daniel.

Daniel now known as Mrs Soti was this smartly dressed middle-aged woman. The hair extensions clipped into a Tony Braxton cut; side short and into a crop. With a few etiquette lessons on how to sit and how to walk she was stunning. Caleb tried to drill Daniel, an apprehensive student of deportment and manners.

The style complimented his diamond shaped face and high cheek bones. Caleb told Daniel to be clean shaven so that he could glue on the wig to avoid any mishaps. No one could figure out it's a wig. It glued onto his bald head and no hairline was out of sorts.

They fought over a manicure treatment which Caleb had to do to give Daniel a feminine appearance. Caleb bought the instant easy to apply false nails for an instant makeover and a pack of false eyelashes. Caleb could easily put the acrylic nails on and off, they came in many different colours. He had to tweeze the eyebrows and plucked hairs in the nose, and of all things; a facial treatment. Cleansing, exfoliating, and toning. Daniel sat through the process with contempt and sheer curiosity.

Caleb wanted things to go easy, he called a private spa professional for Daniel. It included a pedicure, waxing and exfoliating to remove the excess hair. The spa treatment gave Caleb a head start so he could tweak Daniel to a feminine touch. The skin was ready for further buffing and light makeup.

Caleb liked the minerals powder and brush in a compact case. It just toned Daniel's skin to a perfect, bronze texture. After much probing and deep cleansing, Daniel was ready for the show of his life.

Caleb sat next to Daniel in the conference room. It was situated next to the presidential suite. Caleb threw a quick look at Daniel with a smirk on his face. Daniel in turn touched his lips checking if they are moist and dabbed a bit of Vaseline. Daniel kept wondering how this man could know so much about women's affairs. He assumed it could have been the training to support a female or male president.

Caleb addressed the meeting and gave the plan of action. He had done his homework and the team knew which areas to focus on.

Caleb leaned closer to Daniel and whispered to him to wipe his brow. It was shiny and greasy. He thought Daniel might be freaking out or that nerves had set in. With a wink, Daniel nearly burst out in his husky voice to tell Caleb to back off. The seven men team was on the roll.

"Your boss has one hell of a husky voice. I hope she is not as bossy as she sounds. She must have too much testosterone. I think she can take on any man." The audit manager Josh laughed as he shared with Caleb when they went to the bathroom.

Poor Daniel struggled when they separated at the entrance to the toilets. He nearly scrambled into 'men's only' to be given a gentle pull by Caleb.

Daniel had a lot to learn as he said earlier, "Caleb the worst is yet to come."

****

Maya always made sure they chatted every night if she is apart from Daniel. Malaysia was their favourite holiday home as it has the same climate as Kush. The flight was less than two hours. Many of Maya's contemporaries were on social media like twitter and Myspace. Maya used an alias name to keep pace with her high-flying circle. She always kept information to a minimum online, realising the complexity of their lifestyle.

"Honey… everything ok" Maya called Daniel on his private line. Still in Kush when are you going, wherever you are going?"

"Hello, darling I am still in and around, up and about Kush. I will text you if I have to be out of the country."

"Dan I had a nice spa and pedicure darling, they always have new products every year. I feel so refreshed and energised."

"Oh… me too dear" Daniel answered with a yawn.

"What! Daniel; did you say, me too?"

"Oh hell no, I said oh my time."

Daniel corrected himself.

"I am fiddling with my mobile dear, it is not setting the alarm."

"Ohm Daniel I heard you right,"

"Are you missing me," Daniel tried to change the topic.

"Maybe that's why I sound like a parrot. I am tired it has been a day of marathon meetings Maya."

"Give my love to the boys, love you and hey do enjoy. Sleep tight, darling."

Daniel went to sit in one of his recliner chairs near the fireplace. At this time of the night in the state House, staff are out of earshot. He liked to read and catch up on foreign affairs and domestic affairs. Daniel realised that this could have been a close shave. He was nearly caught by Maya. Daniel asked himself what made him do such a drastic metamorphosis?

He never had a chance in his life to be adventurous in his own way with Caleb, his pal from high school to Harvard. Being able to click and be a carry-on, they never found the opportunity.

As an adolescent, he always spent his time herding the goats and cows. He was either in school or many holidays in a book sitting in the pastures. The chores around the house were many, cutting wood, fixing a fence and feeding cows, chickens goats and sheep. Going to school in the village was a painstaking task, ten miles to and fro.

The first time to be on his own was when he went to Harvard. Harvard was an environment of an educational keeping up appearances and not home turf. They could not afford to have boys will be boys' adventure.

It was all serious study and alien socialisation but they trotted on and adjusted as much as they could. With their brains, it was plain sailing and they could challenge fellow students to any debate. It was the usual University shenanigans which they missed; like doing things on their own terms. In America, Caleb and Daniel saw how people of colour had to be careful in public. Lest they are accused of any crime.

Caleb and Daniel stayed away from clubbing, gatherings and fraternities and even the final leaver's party.

The favourite place was a local café just outside the University and a visit to a friend that they met on the plane from Kush. He was from Bongo and his family was settled in the States.

They worked part-time jobs on the campus at the café making enough to cover basics. With the pressure of exams and work, time did sail so quick for the two. It was a stable life and cocooned from crime.

They survived five years of gruelling grafting and studying to achieve their first-class degrees and a Ph.D. Caleb always said that opportunity cost worked in their favour. It was either to have fun and possibly be in prison. Or this recluse University life with focus; the later had done them well.

Mrs Doubt on Fire

"Ouch! My bunion hurts Caleb, I need sandals, the court shoes pressed on my corn. Get me those plasters from the pharmacy." Daniel removed his shoes with a moan and slumped himself on the sofa.

"Do not worry. I have you covered." Caleb took out a pair of flat sandals with straps to cover the toes comfortably.

"Much better." Daniel sat on the bed in the Presidential suite in preparation for the first assignment.

"We are meeting with the Minister of Finance Mr Skamu. The audit team will get there in time. They know what to do and are expecting us; so for us it's fact-finding."

"The helicopter will be on standby to whisk us out to the rural areas. I have covered all the three provinces. In the process, we can target our audit on health, agriculture, education, industry and technology."

Daniel quickly put on a lovely lilac dress, he settled for dresses. Two-piece power dressing was too much of an inconvenience for him in the bathroom. The pencil skirt was a nightmare to pull up.

"Can you please talk slowly, your voice modulation is too high. If you slow down, no one will bother with your husky voice."

Poor Daniel it was more than he bargained for.

"No lipstick Caleb, I will use Vaseline, I always touch my mouth it will smudge everywhere."

"It's the X chromosome that is in me, now revealing itself. What has gone wrong with me I look like a woman? It has to take a cross-dressing President to know the goings-on in his country, this is crazy stuff."

Daniel inspected himself in the mirror and could barely see the man he was. A woman stood right in front of him. No hairs out of place, goatee all gone and the nails looked pristine.

"Is this the cost of loving my country?"

"Okay, let's hit the road Jack, and paint the whole town red." Caleb ran a quick check and gave thumbs up.

"Oh how funny." Daniel moaned as he struggled with his handbag zipper which was caught on a tissue paper.

The Minister of Finance Jacob Skamu is a middle-aged man of fifty and known for his Casanova antics. After one look at Daniel he gave a wink then went to sit in his chair. Wanting to take charge, Daniel reminded Skamu that this was a serious exercise to benefit both parties.

He stressed that it would forge a way forward in information technology. Daniel talked about efficient internal control systems and work ethics.

Skamu bolted up and gave Daniel red chilli eye as if he had a hangover.

"Listen here Soti, I am the boss you do not come here and start to tell me what to do. I am the man and do not take kindly to woman orders whoever you might be. I will say exactly how things will run. Whether you are from Daniel house or Kush House, the buck stops right here, get it! If you dare harass my staff, you will be hearing from me. The media or the party is not too kind either."

Jacob Skamu walked to the side table and poured some water and drank noisily.

"Do you want me to put you through to the president's phone?" Daniel interrupted Skamu.

"I have his adviser Caleb right here. You know Caleb and the President are personally interested in the findings to help us, as a country to move forward."

"He knows it is not easy for everyone to be compliant to 21st-century technology. It needs foreign currency and human resources. Our human resources are living the country going abroad." Daniel kept talking.

"Well not so fast madam, just stay clear of my personal details and check systems only okay. Done deal, good luck Soti."

"You are one heck of a woman if say, Ohm. Ten years younger I could be waltzing you to strictly go dancing.

Got to go tootle do guys. I have a lunch meeting with the investor guys from Sweden. We have to take care of them to take care of us. If you know what I mean."

"Hick, hick, hick, so cheerio guys."

Skamu left the meeting and the team of seven was gobsmacked to see such contempt for authority. The audit manager was a professional internal auditor. He appeared not fazed to see such behaviour in government ministries.

Ignorant staff equated audits to a witch hunt and never thought of the benefits of the findings. Staff in some departments tried to bribe the audit team to write favourable reports. This made auditing a failed pursuit in itself. It was a sombre moment for Daniel to realise that contempt and unprofessional behaviour can come from his top aides. No acknowledgement of positive professional ethics. Daniel saw scorn throughout the meeting. On top of that an immediate write-off of Mrs Soti, a well groomed and educated woman. This included a wink and leaking of lips.

Daniel shivered.

"Ohm, way to go Caleb." he shouted. They looked at each other and raised their arms in defeat. The rest of the team went about their first audits. The two cronies waited for a helicopter to take them to the first league of their rural meeting.

Undercover Sting Operation

Caleb had done his preparation for the next meeting. Agricultural extension officers, farmers and locals gathered at a school assembly hall in Chenga Mission. The security team made sure it is strictly no media or journalists. The smart team hovered in the air and below to make sure the operation was according to specifications. Caleb asked the helicopter team to land away from the school to enable Daniel to compose himself. The team wanted Daniel taken in a car to the school.

This event did not go unnoticed as the locals heard about this extraordinary meeting in their mission school. The school kids ran as fast as they could to the mission school. They expected some food handouts or just anything to eat. The elders overheard children gossiping about a man and a woman dropped by a helicopter.

The chief was an elderly man wearing the full traditional garb holding a lion's tail. He was not in a hurry as he greeted the people coming to sit at the front tables. The people sat down and listened to the chief as he ranted on about problems in the village. Caleb and Mrs Soti sat in front with the rest of the leaders. With a hand on his cheek, Daniel (Mrs Soti) sat looking bored. He was at the same time compromising his posture by sitting with his legs slightly separate.

After the chief's protocol, Caleb stood up and introduced him-self-and the rest of the delegates. When it came to Daniel, Caleb forgot and said,

"I want like to introduce you to Mrs Daniel." There was total silence and people started whispering and talking to themselves. Daniel quickly pulled Caleb and told him,

"It's Mrs Soti."

"Apologies, I meant Mrs Soti," Caleb tried to correct the situation.

One elder abruptly rose and pointed at Daniel,

"You do look like the President's sister and how and why we do not know. Anyway, can you madam sit properly like a woman of dignity. Who are you for real, you come here and have no manners sitting like a man?"

"Is this what education is doing to our children?" The crowd was hysterical.

Security personnel went and asked the man to sit down. The crowd roared with laughter. It took a while to control the crowd, it was more like a stand-up comedy gone wrong.

The extension officers talked of not having any support with funds to buy motorbikes to reach the remote villages. Locals complained of not getting help from the government.

Farmers wanted the government to help them with transport and give extension officers motorbikes to reach remote areas.

They complained of a lack of seeds and no one explaining to them about the new crop called genetically modified. The local farmers were afraid to be used as Ginny pigs.

They complained that no one told them about the implications of using Genetically Modified crops. They were afraid of what their children were telling them about having deformities. One farmer testified that a farm five miles away had accepted to grow a GMO crop. The farmer was given seeds for free and his plantation is now under cultivation. The local farmers wanted to do crop rotation and use manure to fertilise their fields. The villagers only saw non–governmental organisations that came to do their projects and were grateful.

The local farmers complained that the government rarely came to follow up on programmes. The foreign workers preferred to stay in cities. The appointed local agents focused more in their own areas and farms. They forgot about the projects that bring public benefit.

Kushians wanted irrigation and boreholes that way they could at first feed their family.

After feeding their families, the peasant farmers sad they can begin to do more and increase acreage.

The villagers only saw government officials during elections. This came as a surprise to see these high-ranking officials come to their village.

The villagers told the officials they want to help themselves but with little or no government help they were helpless. A village chief stood up.

"Honourable guests we thank you for coming to see us in this remote village. Can someone here tell me what a government is there for?"

"Is the President the mayor of Edom capital or the President of Kush? Please tell the President to subdivide the country because the only place that is governed is Edom Capital?"

"I have no education and going to my grave not able to read and write. Wisdom tells me that we have a problem with our leaders. If you cannot run the whole country why waste time coming here to address us. Life in the villages is tough we need help to help ourselves. We did not choose to live in this barren land."

"After centuries of living under siege like animals in our own land. We have no government help to create communities that can propel us to better our lives. Whom are we waiting for and from where to say_ Go ahead yes it's your land, it's your country rule yourself?"

"Who is in control of this country? Do we still have some invisible control from somewhere" The old man was agitated?

Children walk to school at least more than 5 miles one-way, many on an empty stomach. The villagers expressed the need to have a government that can focus on rural development.

They wanted help to create communities but still keeping the village appeal. The villagers thought that water, electricity and housing can be located in a central place for a greater good. The scattered homesteads were an impediment to rural development.

Daniel knew what they were talking about. Not having water sources for home use, taking water from the river infested with bacteria. The long journeys to school, no lunch box or books and pencils.

Daniel made sure that his family is taken care of before he came back to Kush. They worked hard in various cafes around Massachusetts. He saved money that is how he managed to support his family in Kush. His sister Sara went to a teaching college and earned a teaching diploma and there after a degree with the Open University. With his hard-earned wages from the part-time job at the university café, he knew it could be much more back home. Daniel was confident that his sister could take care of business while he is away, including legal and financial affairs.

Sara, his sister, obliged and built a lovely homestead on an open veld in a farming area in Mase.

The farm was fenced, trees, shrubs and flowers planted to make it beautiful. They bought a small apartment in the city to enable parents to visit the Doctors and do some shopping.

When Daniel became president getting labourers was not an issue. Daniel's parents were from humble beginnings they were thankful to God that their son could provide for them. The opportunity to get a better education abroad brought jealousy from the neighbours. They were peasant farmers and as the Simba family became prosperous, they bought a bigger farm and became fully fledged farmers. The Simbas in their 80s they still milked the cows.

They could still do some jobs on the farm; despite the many workers provided by Daniel. They started specialising in dairy cows and citrus fruits for export; kept a small patch of garden for corn and other family vegetable needs.

Daniel saw the evidence that if Kushians are given direction and know how; the sky can be the limit. Daniel loved fishing so a man- made lake was dug and it did keep him entertained when he visited the farm. Clean water supplies, beautiful chalets, enough food in the garden, kept his parents content and transformed.

Some of Daniel's contacts came to visit from overseas and went hunting on the vast acreage. Sara was in charge of hospitality and an efficient manager. She saw to the needs of the foreign visitors.

The family did its part to find conservation methods to keep up with changing weather patterns. They recycled and planted trees to replace old ones and kept their front areas covered with lawn and beautiful flowers.

One could see potted plants of Kush violets lined on the window seal.

Marigolds, justice, dragon snaps on the front pouch and bougainvillaea's lined all the way to the orchards. This was a world in Kush not seen by many. A Kushian just living in a clean and organically inspired environment; away from wars and tribal fights.

****

Caleb set up a primary school's exchange programme. He invited rural schools within the catchment area to come and share ideas.

Caleb funded the meeting from the president's budget. His idea was to bring teachers and school children from the various remote schools to come together. The schools planned to compete in debates and sports.

The President wanted to see the ordinary people that always support his party come rain or sunshine. The government provided minibuses to bring the children and teachers to the meeting place at Papaya school.

The teachers had no idea that a government official was going to be there. The meeting enabled Caleb and Daniel to mix and mingle with the kids and teachers. Daniel watched as the kids were milling around chatting with their counterparts.

Mr Maru a head teacher came and started chatting with Mrs Soti (Daniel). The noise from the crowd made it impossible to talk.

Daniel asked the head teacher to walk away from the crowd to hear each other speak.

"How long have you been a Principal Sir," Daniel asked his new acquaintance.

"Well madam over thirty-five years of service, things have been the same since. Yes, a little bit of progress in the government offices where we have our own people. It is a good thing, but down here in the roots nothing much."

"We struggle with everything. Now the President has stopped free education in rural areas, so it is a sad state of affairs. Poor helpless people madam, who have a Government as their hope get nothing. The soil is not giving, the rains are not coming and the money cannot be made. Above all the government does not care whether we are here or not."

"It takes the spirit out of every Kush patriot to keep up appearances in these woods. The only thing Simba could have done is to give the rural areas a chance and let them pick up. We are one nation and can boost small businesses here to sustain ourselves."

Principal Maru was a defeated man. He looked at Mrs Soti and just nodded his head.

"The government needs to look inwards and not expect all of us to do the great trek overseas. What does it take for a President to say stuff it? Enough of protocols let us save the next generation?"

"Most people live here in rural areas and many were settled on dry arid land by the settlers. How much more suffering can they take when our government keeps mum and thinks we are just going to turn out alright?"

"We need stationery, books and food programmes to feed the kids, they come from their homes on empty stomachs. It's the sheer craving for knowledge that keeps them coming to schools. Some faint and it is upsetting."

"I respect your honesty, Sir. We are relying on you; do not give up hope. Our children are the future and they want you to keep up the good spirit."

As the two separated to get some refreshments, Simba reflected. To him, it was deeply disturbing that nothing had changed much since his school days. Many kids come to school on empty stomachs.

Those that could bring cheek peas and maize cobs, they shared as much as they could. Just a few grains to keep the others focused. Some children went into the forest to look for edible fruits and berries and some looking for termites.

A little girl was scratching words on the ground, her face covered with tears. Simba knelt beside her and drew a happy face. The little girl looked up and stared at Simba.

"Why do you draw a happy face, I am not happy I am never happy, I miss my mum and dad," Daniel took the girl's hand and went to sit on a bench.

"How old are you little one, you have beautiful eyes."

"My name is Tanya I am seven years old my mum died of aids. I have a bigger brother he is now 10 years and helps me to come to school."

"Who is taking care of you then, anyone older to see to your needs child?"

"Ohm, its different people in the village at times come to check on us but they are not keen. They say they do not want to catch the disease. That is why I am always by myself no one wants to play with me. They just come and throw food items and we have to cook for ourselves."

"Father was working in town in a factory he got sick and mum also became sick and died."

"My brother tries to look for firewood and goes fishing in the river far away. Sometimes he misses school and washes my clothes. They all call me dirty Tanya because I have no uniform and my clothes smell."

"My teacher tries to help and take me to her house every week to give me a wash, she at times gives me her children's old clothes madam."

"How did you come to school today, child?" Daniel was running out of words to describe such pain from a child.

"Ohm, we walk a lot, my brother carries me and he is not patient because I have no shoes. I hurt myself with thorns look here I have an abscess on my big toe… Ouch, it hurts it is about to burst."

This was the time the little girl poured a watershed of tears hidden behind years of tough interior. It was rare for Tanya to find someone who could take this time to listen to her. This woman with expensive clothes and smelt nice sat with her and talked with her for 30 minutes.

She seemed interested in her. She cried her little heart out. A teacher seeing the commotion came to Daniel's aid.

"Miss, please get me a 1st aid box this girl needs help she has an abscess on her big toe."

"Are you her relative do you know who she is? It is Tanya the girl that lost her parents and you would not want to deal with that boil if I were you."

Daniel was so enraged he called in his loud male voice to Caleb.

He shouted and brought the whole conference to a standstill. Daniel's adam's apple jutted out like a stuck oxtail bone. They thought he had a demon and the poor girl wiped her tears quickly. She went into shock when Daniel blasted her eardrums. Caleb was tucked in the truck he could not stand the hot weather. When he heard the bellowing call, he quickly jumped out and ran to his President's aid.

"Get me the 1st aid box in the car and attend to this girl. She has a boil it's now sceptic and needs attention now, get some Paracetamol too. Get some Epson salts from my briefcase, it will help relieve the pain."

Caleb ran like a sports champion to the car and brought the box to dress up the boil.

After much confusion, the little girl trusted Caleb to clean her toe. He cleaned and applied the Epson salt with a dressing and Paracetamol to help her pain. Tanya was smitten by this kind attention from this woman she had never met before. It was the first time in her life anyone had taken time. In her mother's house at 4 years, she could pick wood and make a fire and fetch water. She was an adult before her time and learnt fast how to take care of herself.

The father was a factory worker in the city and rumoured to have a second wife with many kids. When dad happened to come home, it was because the city wife was tired of taking care of him and wanted some time off. This was the last journey home for Tanya's father.

The mother did not take long and followed her dear husband that was never at home to the grave.

Tanya could not believe her luck having a group of people fussing over her today. She was given a drink and some scones. She took a plastic paper from the ground and wrapped tight, half her scone and half the drink. Daniel did not miss this gesture and asked Tanya.

"Why are you not finishing your drink Tanya and your scone there is more. We can go and buy you more food if you want, please eat."

"My brother cannot walk, he is sick. I have to take care of him I cannot eat this food by myself its wrong, its wrong."

"We have to share I have to share with my brother so that he comes back to school."

Tanya was back to her wailing again.

Daniel was so affected by this sad state of affairs. He wondered how many are going through this life without anyone doing something about it. The community was so poor, the fact that the kids tried to come to school touched Daniel's heart.

Caleb looked for the teacher that Tanya mentioned and they went to a private room to talk with her. Daniel could not be drawn into further discussion his shouting drama had caused enough stares. He was emotional after meeting Tanya. He knew Caleb would do the right things.

"Tanya told us about the help you have been giving her. I am from the government and work with the President. I want to ask you to help us, help Tanya and her brother. Her brother needs to be in the hospital. Is it okay if we give you the support you need to help them to have some order in their lives?"

"Aids cannot be transmitted by just touching it is through contact with blood and bodily fluids. Tanya knows you, and it would be horrendous for her to see strange people in her life right now."

"Please, whatever you need we shall pay you as their carer. We will make sure she gets school uniforms and stationery, we will give you the money. We shall leave everything in your capable hands can you please put in all your details."

"One of our officers from social services will come and see that you have room for Tanya next to your homestead. Tanya will not need to travel far to get to school. I will have a chat with the head teacher. They need to know how aids is transmitted."

"They must not ostracise our children and communities."

"Here's is some basic upkeep for Tanya, please take her to your home. We will ask the hospital to send an ambulance for her brother."

The teacher was grateful of this windfall from Caleb and assured him that Tanya will be safe.

Caleb went and sat under a Mopani tree and watched the children and teachers mix and mingle. The innocence of the kids and the free-spirited noises made him smile. The dedication on the teacher's faces was obvious as they tried to make sense of a meeting that brought them together. Each school made a commitment to make this a yearly event.

The teachers were committed despite the deep problems that beset the rural land.

The teachers took their profession seriously and respected their authorities. Each teacher came with a passion for sharing and learning. Making sure that the children entrusted to them are safe and enjoying this once in a lifetime gathering.

"At least we can smile amid disastrous and horrendous life happenings Caleb. Tanya haunts my soul. How can anyone survive under such conditions?"

"She came to school today, her brother is ill and she has a septic boil. She is hungry and she cannot walk far and she has no parents."

"The extent of the suffering is making me weak. I cannot do anything I cannot solve this problem called Kush, Caleb."

****

On their way towards his home area, Daniel viewed the vast expanse of his country and the extent of his reign. These seemingly single individual experiences had shown him a greater picture of the devastating effects of poverty.

"My country is rich in minerals resources, why are we poor. Where has all the mineral money gone to? The glaring disparities between rural lives and Kush city life is just wide."

"It's the government sitting on its laurels armed with archaic laws, and out of date principles that have no bearing on Kush."

"A government by the people for the people has the mandate to instil a vision by creating working communities."

Daniel's mind ran wild as he thought about the challenges of running a Kush government.

National Health Service

Edom General Hospital is situated five miles from the city centre. The public transport system is mainly the emergency taxis which are seen plying the major routes in the cities and towns. Many times on the hospital highway, ambulances are a regular presence. They speed picking up pedestrians and passengers run over by the manic taxi-drivers. They race and compete to collect the sick casualties to and from hospitals.

Caleb was ready to take Daniel (Mrs Soti) to visit the major hospital in Edom capital city as the next assignment. He arranged in advance with the hospital department heads. They met the chief consultant Doctor Dena, an elderly Kushian, who had worked at the hospital for 30 years and manages his own clinics around the city. He was happy to lead the team and show them around the hospital, giving them an outline of the situation.

A visit from the Presidential team was indeed a rare treat, Dena wanted the truth to be told. Dena made it clear that the situation had changed for the worst since the privatisation introduced by President Daniel Simba. People were failing to pay for basic treatments.

The corridors were full of sick people in agony and waiting to be seen by anyone medically trained. Some patients were covered in blood, wreathing in pain.

"You obviously have to be well to come to this place. The sick seem to be in the wrong place." Daniel thought aloud.

In the corridor, a nurse came up to Dena

"Dr Dena sir we have might have to stop working we have run out of gloves, and operations booked tomorrow will have to be cancelled."

Dena wanted to reply but decided to keep it to himself realising that this was just the tip of the ice bag.

"Caleb; remember me its Ron from Mase mission come on Mr Adviser I always bit you at maths."

Caleb was still wondering, "Oh Ron what's up with you." Caleb had to stop and be civil.

"Got aids man, from blood transfusion it was discovered late, so it's a day by day survival. I was involved in car accident, a taxi-driver rammed behind me and I skidded off into a gully."

Caleb put his arm on Ron's shoulder.

"Oh no Ron sorry."

"It is a tough man: I am not working now, lost my job and depend on charity funding to get the antiretroviral drugs it's tough going.

"What about food Ron."

"Well, its family and friends." Ron looked down.

Caleb took out some paper money placed in Ron's hands and gave him his number.

"Ron, please call me; I have to go, we are on an assignment."

Daniel wanted to sob but held himself.

"People expect the government to help them than to wait for the international community."

Daniel took out a tissue to blow his nose it was just overwhelming for him and the smell from the morgue. Doctor Dena told Daniel that people are failing to collect their dead because they have not cleared hospital debts.

"It is worse when the electricity goes off, many times. We have load-shedding so it's touch-and-go." Dena continued.

They met a woman crying frantically, her child had died and she was pregnant. The husband left for South Africa to look for work. She could not afford to pay the fees for the operation.

Daniel was now seen wiping tears and he asked Doctor Dena why they could not be compassionate with such cases.

"Ma'am this is a daily occurrence and everyone needs help. We might as well turn this hospital into a charity to accommodate all these sad situations."

Dena led the two cronies into his office, Daniel had seen enough suffering.

"If we do not ask for the money the government stops the grants. The rest of the people lose out on services, the budget is meagre. The private clinics and some hospitals are for the rich and famous."

"The computer system is not compliant to have an online inventory. It is all guesswork and see I have just been told today that we have no gloves. Simple, gloves; that is how bad it is. The staff is leaving for greener pastures and it goes on and on. How do we solve a problem like this?"

"It is a never-ending crisis management. The people now realise that Daniel is an alien puppet. He has brought in a system that will use, abuse us and eventually throw us out of existence. A real Kleptocrats who dines with his sponsors the plutocracy. I am an intellectual and can see where they are coming from." Dena carried on.

"Capitalism has not worked, it is a formula that is meant to keep the rich richer and poor poorest. Globally the poorest, in theory, are the African countries. Hence, wars, dictators and everything else brewed in a foreign cauldron pot to make sure we do not make anything of ourselves."

"Kush is rich in minerals, like oil and gases still unexplored. If a Kushian owns such resources its black diamond and blood money. Black gold, or blood this and blood that. This is so, so that no one buys and then privately it's looted in clandestine operations. Zero returns for Kush."

"Madam sorry that you came at such a time when the country is going through a rough patch. It's made worse by this President Daniel Simba. He seems hell-bent on theory than practical politics.

It is meeting the needs of the people? People want food, water, shelter and clothing. It's pure politics, then the people can get up and be counted. With good leadership in control and bona fide leadership, not these United Corporation puppets."

"We need a strong army and police. Most of the time security is there to protect only a few than the nation. The government should employ more soldiers and police details to secure our borders so that we monitor our security."

"Everything is played reverse jive in Kush government. Hence why mercenaries come and go and give guns to vulnerable people to kill each other, it's sick politics."

Doctor Dena looked relaxed and not aware that he is speaking to the President.

"You are sweating a lot madam have I upset you", Dena looked at Daniel.

"No, not at all Doctor, it's just disturbing that's all. It's how we are dehumanising ourselves even to the grave."

Daniel fidgeted on the chair. Dena went through the health statistics, mortality rate, and life expectancy ratios. He put the survival rate at forty-five years.

"The diseases which are now treatable are now wiping the population, like malaria, whooping cough and TB."

"Madam and you Caleb go and tell the President that some of the tablets and medical equipment in use is not to spec. Our lab did a sample test on some antiretroviral drugs they are just chalk dust, madam. It is sad how some people manage this disease; it's placebo effect I suppose. The fake medical drugs scandal is so serious, a swipe through many pharmacies will reveal a lot. This is another crisis on a burdened continent. It is not a media report or exaggeration by foreign media, these are my hospital records.

"If this is happening in the city; what about the remote villages how are they coping?" Daniel asked Dena.

"Forget about the rural areas madam. Rogue people come and do as they please it's a medical testing ground for many clandestine rogue medical companies. The government is not aware of the real issues that affect the ordinary people. Some Ministers take bribes to allow medical tests and experiments on poor people."

"We do have some few bona fide missionary doctors. A rogue missionary Doctor came to Mora mission hospital last year. He was busy carrying out medical tests using controversial drugs banned overseas.

The medical experiment had been rejected by the medical council. They declined testing on humans and animals. The Doctor went ahead, quietly doing the rounds and injecting the innocent people."

"Our hospital posted an intern for further training, everything was unravelled. He discovered that about 100 people had died of swelling of the stomach and sudden loss of sight."

"So madam; rural areas are everyone's play centre. They are so thankful having people come from near far and wide to help them. Anything that can give hope is much appreciated even poison. No one gets to know." Dena responded aloud.

"The rural folks are barely surviving they quietly disappear the same way they came on this earth no one cares."

"It's the same with mineral rich areas suddenly we hear about rebels. It's the international media that knows more about them. Then bam!. Wham. There is fighting in the areas and some unknown people are busy getting minerals from the area."

"We see the fancy state of the art helicopters and equipment and land rovers in these fighting zones and the government cannot match these intruders. I have heard of some people saying the government accents to unknown people coming in to keep order. What a circus they are the mercenaries sponsoring the rebels. Shooting the locals and getting the diamonds out using private jets.

Corruption of the highest order. Stupid, stupid government."

"But I was born in a village." Daniel was visibly shaking.

Kush Mine Disaster

President Daniel; now Mrs Soti and Caleb passed through a mine tributary on their way to the village in Mase. As the free market economy took a grip on Kush. The indigenous Kushians wanted a taste of the mineral pie. They tried not to be left behind in the gold and ore rush. They were using any means necessary to compete with established international conglomerates. Many makeshift tents and plastics are sprawling everywhere where the indigenous miners can scrap a living.

The smell of human waste from the outskirts of the mine tributary was intoxicating. Daniel was puzzled why they could not organise proper sanitation areas. These were a small group of miners: mining ore and using every possible tool to extract ore from the underground. Caleb called out to a young boy that was eating dry cold cornmeal by the rock. Daniel went and sat on the rock next to this young boy and started talking to him.

"Careful madam you will ruin your special clothes. Ma'am, what brings you to these dirty and dangerous places in your high fashion?"

"This is a man's world and fights can erupt any time. Where are you coming from? Do you want to deal and buy some of our mineral ore its good grade, our spec these days is between 39 and 45%?"

The young boy was a chatterbox and carried on munching his dry cob and swiping the flies.

"The ore belt and seam where we are mining these days is good. It's just the transport costs and the company we supply to that can be a real pain. The machines which they use to do assays make mistakes and at times it is deliberate to just undercharge us. If they reject the chrome ore, we still have to pay for the process, so madam this is a black man's dog-eat-dog business."

"The waiting and payday can be a nightmare, no one cares. We at times go and wait for days to just get the payments processed, it's a wait and see game. Our life is in the company's hands, at times they demand bribes just to get our material assayed."

The boy was clever and a smart chatterbox.

"How old are you son?" Daniel asked.

"I am only twelve year's ma'am, my name is Isaiah."

"What! Daniel looked at the boy, stuttering.

"Twelve! Why are you not at school?"

"Well it's a long story, I do go to school, during school time. I go half-day to keep my job here. I come here to work, they send me to the dangerous holes because I am small, to put dynamite. It is frightening. I have to work and at times I can get fifty dollars."

"I pay fifteen dollars for my shares in the group to buy wheelbarrows and stuff. Twenty-five dollars for my parents and ten dollars for my school fees. My mum has to sort out my brothers because I give them everything anyway."

Daniel and Caleb stared fixated on this enigma, a young boy with skills of a 50-year old man.

"I just hope Ma'am I can do well in school, work hard and just be better than this. I love my parents they are now sick and homebound. Papa has tuberculosis because of the asbestos he inhaled at Shaba Asbestos mine."

"Mama worked in the big tobacco plantation. They use, I think DDT some chemical without any protection. She coughs and her skin madam is like a crocodile. She scratches and it piles up at night madam. It's a horrible sight to see her scratch and scratch every night. Can you imagine all that on your smart clothes ma'am?"

"So you are the breadwinner son." Daniel was almost in tears.

"Yes ma'am, I pray that one day maybe our government can look at us and just help us to be better. I want to go to school full-time, I am good but life can be tough. I am good at maths, I help these old thick heads to check the payments and calculations."

"Madam, have you ever gone hungry or ever been without food for months; where you have to look for wild fruits and wild leaves to just boil and eat."

"If I am President I would preside over the whole country, not the cities and his village only. My President is cool he is an educated man. He went to Harvard, he came from somewhere around here. I want to be like him but I want to help all Kushians. He is brainy and hope one day he can help us all to have better villages with electricity, water and shelter."

Many of the adult miners were worry of people in smart cars. They tried to avoid contact and kept away from Daniel and Caleb. Their future in such ventures is not guaranteed income as the government is always changing laws. The old men kept Isaiah their guinea pig chatting as they dug as much as they could. The government never attends to their plight but brings in soldiers to keep law and order. Any protest is met with bloodshed and no apologies.

The miners started shouting the boy's name and cussing him to come quickly to pile the ore into the wheelbarrows. He was a dartboard for sure, as they all called out in frustration. They had many orders he had to do. Grown man all aiming at this poor little boy, still an adolescent.

"What a palaver," Daniel whispered.

Caleb quickly tucked an envelope in Isaiah's big oversized tracksuit pocket as if adjusting his shirt. He told him to keep the money safe and go to school. The big bellied man shouted again for Isaiah they wanted him to set up dynamite.

"What did those slick city people want?" The big bellied man was heckling Isaiah.

"They are not from this area so they were just asking for directions."

Isaiah adjusted his trousers and small torch to prepare for the dark journey into a tunnel where no man had gone before.

****

Vencor International platinum mine is just a few miles from the ore tributary where Daniel and Caleb had just left. Daniel thought about the situation at the ore tributary, the deplorable site.

Individuals groups were scrapping bits and pieces of ore to try to make a living. The miners feared the government and the actions of some ministers who lay claim on the tributaries.

Vencor Platinum mine is a big massive mining operation owned by an International company. At the entrance heavily armed men in uniforms stand at the gates. Caleb produced his visitor's I.D and the guards let them in. The managing director took them on a tour of the mine. The machinery and equipment are to a high specification.

On a tour underground, the workers were busy managing the conveyor belts. Daniel and Caleb had a chance to see the big conveyor belts as they brought the mineral from beneath the earth. The top hierarchy is foreign and a few blacks in Administration, Human Resources and Accounting.

A tour of the mine compounds showed a shocking revelation. It was just tin huts in a row and ablution blocks right at the end of the poor buildings. These were the people Daniel wanted to meet.

"Do you have school facilities and a clinic?" Daniel asked a skinny old woman they met outside the compound.

"No, we go to a small clinic in the village the doctor comes once a fortnight. It's run by a nursing aid from the donors."

"If we want more help we go to the city. The company does not provide schools. We have to send our kids to the village school five miles away." The woman could barely stand.

"We have a mine company shop. We buy stuff on credit and most of us are deep in debt, our husband's wages are tied up already."

The woman was gaunt and weary; carrying a baby on her back. She balanced a bucket of water on her head and looked pregnant. The message was the same. The company has a Corporate Social Responsibility to see to the welfare of the miners.

The company had it written in their HQ mission statement but it applied on paper, not on Kush mine workers.

As things were, it was the same story, the poor have no one to speak and advocate for them. The mine made sure they are hooked, hook line and soul to their mine.

With food debts and school fee loans, the families did not have much to live by. Daniel had seen enough and wanted to escape to his old village and see if anything had changed.

Welcome To The Woods

Daniel felt melancholic visiting the village where he was born. The old rugged, dusty roads and huts had not changed. The small huts here and there were still there to mark a place of residence. He bought a farm for his parents, 40 miles away on the highway to the city. They had come unannounced and people were wondering whom they were.

The dust road to the homestead was fraught with potholes and rocks. Small kids with no clothes were chasing the car to the homestead where Daniel grew up. Behind them, a trail of dust brought with it a tornado of whirlwind. Daniel's cousins on the father's side came to settle on the homestead.

Caleb introduced Daniel as a friend of President Simba. The villagers knew Caleb he used to visit the farm with President Daniel.

"We are just passing by and felt an urge to come and see how you are doing. We will pass on the message to President Simba, he expects us to. He would be upset to know that we are in the area and failed to see you." Caleb tried to keep a straight face.

"Come in", the old woman welcomed the cronies into the kitchen.

A small fire burning was in the grass thatched kitchen and the smoke was just unbearable. Without a chimney, the smoke spread inside the kitchen hut. Caleb politely asked the old lady if they could sit outside. Daniel started coughing hard he was almost choking. The deep croaking cough was as if it's from a buffalo's belly.

"Oh, my word; daughter you cough like a possessed maniac. I have some medicine to cure that. Are you married, such a rumbling noise can surely put a man off, child?" The old woman could talk for the whole village.

"Ohm… Are you sure that you not related to the Simbas? Something is nagging me that you are of our own kind, come closer my daughter. You somehow look like the Simbas but you got some powerful scent about you. I was not born yesterday you know. The daughter of my cousins Sara she was just little she now teaches at a city college; you are a spitting image." The old woman kept talking nonstop; she stood up and started dancing.

"One of us once lost is here," She went on as the family looked at her with utter confusion.

"A child of this soil is here to connect with the umbilical cord she left, went far away and now is back to her home."

She started ululating and the other villagers dancing around them.

"Oh my; my; did my cousin have children without letting us know? You are a Simba and I feel it in my bones. Boys get a chicken and kill it now, one of ours is here. We shall let them know when we call at the President's farm, what is hiding is now out, our other daughter is back from afar."

Daniel just kept up with the drama he could not put a word through. She was in charge and the whole village agreed. The old woman started mumbling something gibberish. She started dancing around the two cronies and Caleb stood nodding his head.

"Complaining of smoke: my foot...Aargh, aha... city people." She grumbled.

Before they could leave, the old woman brought plates with food.

"Oh no!" Daniel protested. It was relish of dried pumpkin leaves with peanut butter, biltong and cornmeal. It was worth the risk; Caleb was almost wiping his plate with his hands. They had not realised how much they missed village cooking; on an open fireplace with clay cooking pots.

"There is a difference when cooking with traditional cookware." Caleb found this intriguing.

Daniel could not a put a finger to it as well.

"Caleb it's like an earth clay pot connecting with the relish which comes from the soil. It's like life in the slow lane with nature as the extravagant experience, worth the venture." They all agreed.

Caleb kept apologising to the old woman that they could not wait for a ceremony. They were passing by and just wanted to greet the family. The old lady slumped on the floor with dejection and started crying. Caleb took out some groceries from the truck and a wad of money. He thanked the woman profusely for her hospitality. She bolted up and hugged the two.

She gave blessings and still insisted that they at least take the chicken and slaughter at their own time.

"It is taboo to reject an offer of Thanksgiving," The old woman chided them.

This was the true love of Kushians, even those with nothing. They can sacrifice the last chicken to cook for a visitor or passer-by. That's what Daniel knew about his culture. How this love could not transcend to communities, government and politics anymore was just a disappointment. Greed, chicanery, scorn, pull him down syndrome and gross manipulation of the weak was now the order of the day.

Daniel knew that people need leadership to guide them to better ways of doing things. Not to just watch, wait and see. Daniel found inspiration in his own heritage.

****

"Dad!" Daniel's son Abel called him from Oxford in the UK. Papa, you cannot believe it. I passed my degree with first-class honours dad."

"Well done young man; so what do you want to do next son, well done, well done my boy."

"I want to be a biophysicist dad; so I have enrolled for a postgrad dad. I will pay from the money I get from my property so do not worry dad.

"Oh no do not do that, you have an educational fund set aside. Leave it to me son, just email the details and I will follow up okay."

"So dad what's up with you; mum says you are not with her in Malaysia. Dad, I am joining her tomorrow. You okay guys, any issues Pa."

"No there is nothing to worry about son; everything is honkey dory. I have to work on an important exercise, before year end. I have to make sure it is done."

"Ohm, you can delegate dad. What is it that can force you not to go with mum, you the President for goodness sake?" Abel sounded worried.

"Son we will talk, but honestly it is important to everyone. I am a father to 15 million, so that's the price."

"It's okay dad, but know what; looking at how much the western world has advanced in science, technology and engineering. Dad, we can now Google any geographical place on earth. They have been to the moon and tried Mars dad. This is just a tip of the iceberg."

"When are we going to have a sense of purpose and divert from tribal wars and personal dislike of each other. We need to focus on things that make our lives better."

"I have moments dad when I wonder in class when other students are talking about this development and that. Africa is left out as a nonentity. Dad something has to change, if it needs prayers, I will do whatever it takes."

"I am proud of my country my people and who we are. Not to squeal when it comes to Africa. Some professors just take the mickey dad. For me, it is worse knowing I am your son."

"Poverty topics they look at us, corruption dad they give Africa as an example. Bad leadership dictators' dad they focus on Africa."

"Europe and the USA have even bigger corruption cases but it's taken as a case study only. How much can a student take knowing the father is at the helm."

"Where do you fit in dad? I know you are a good man but they paint us all with the same brush dad. Every ill wind in the world they say it's African. If economies fail in the West, they never blame anyone they bail out dad. At times, it's deliberate blaming and its becoming outrageous and we are allowing it" Abel was distraught.

"That is a good question son, who is them? If you cannot, point a finger at the perpetrator of these accusations. Son, you just do what you destined to achieve in the circumstances you are."

"Do it well and you do not have to prove anything to anyone. Kush is ever ready for its sons and daughters to come and give back their expertise so home is waiting for you son. Tell everyone it's all of us who have to make things happen. Black-and-white patriotic Kushians, not the President alone you hear" Daniel thought about this new emerging Abel, a different kind of man.

"I have tried to keep a rap on it, dad, I do not want this taunting every day. How much time do we have to wait for divine providence? Mum preaches about it always, dad? You are the president can you not make a change dad."

"I question my faith daily why I have to be the laughing stock of International Relations. Why God is not allowing us to have a good life just like the first world. How can I enjoy my success when everyone else is left behind, it's not sweet dad its sour."

"Keep your head son and well done, you have never taken your wealth for granted. Love you son."

Daniel's thoughts took him to that bright young boy of twelve working in a dangerous mine. The boy is used to put dynamite, no protective clothing and not much to eat. The old man bullying him, the frustrations of mine ventures based on maybes. He took out a handkerchief; tears were coming out uncontrollably. Daniel knew the boy is bright can talk in detail.

He knew about chrome ore specifications the costing and became a breadwinner at twelve years.

"The people need opportunities a twelve-year-old has shown me. Africans are not dumb its lack of bona fide leadership."

"Things were becoming too much to grasp as people are just barely surviving. They have no plans, no vision because of lack of government backing. How do they answer the reason for existing" Daniel's thoughts started to wonder?

Moment Of Realisation

"I cannot carry on Caleb, I am hurting it is just too much for me. I am overwhelmed my friend. It's like carrying the weight of Kush on my shoulders."

"Free market systems have taken out morality, ethics and virtues in governance. It's a dog-eat-dog, an Apprentice-style TV programme of business conduct, with no mercy. Capitalism has failed flat on its face. We need new economic theories that can encompass all the economic activities, without short-changing the poor."

"A system that looks at the weak and strong. Like a SWOT analysis of economics using one another equitably. We are a human species that creates wealth which oppress the labourer or poor."

"Caleb I can rant on about the way of the world. It is the state of my Kush that is draining my soul. We are allowing our children to be used as advertising material, by possibly well intentioned external organisations."

"Small kids with boogies and in so much pain, paraded as world spectacles. Shut the camera down take wipes and clean up the kid! Get a bottle of water and give the hungry children."

"Why watch the kids dying or collecting dirty infested water? Caleb where are we in all this. Abroad on a yacht."

Caleb came over to Daniel and gave him a good bear hug. Daniel sobbed like a baby and let go to sit in his swivel chair.

"I am grateful to you Caleb we procrastinated a venture that was worth the risk. This was no kid's adventure my friend. If Machiavellian intelligence meant us to retrogress as a people. It surely needed us to take a stupid stunt like this."

"We could not grasp this in a Kush bubble house. It's so easy to be complacent and accept the status quo despite the obviously constipated existence of Kush."

"Caleb it might easily be seen as child's play, but thank God we have started this, let's finish it. I want to see the end of it mate. I am stronger now and will sob no more."

"The young boy, the young pregnant woman, fake drugs, Tanya, Aids scourge, corruption where are we in all this Caleb. This is a travesty of justice, who is there to correct these differences, my friend."

"Are you sure Daniel you will not crack up again because you have been a trooper? Blacks look odd in drag and makeovers, but you are just perfect."

Daniel looked at Caleb with gratitude.

"Evil prevails if good men do nothing so it's said." Daniel put on his jacket and they walked out of the basement office.

****

"Anyone in, good people. I am just passing by to check my document; the Chinese deal."

Dumbo came to Kush House struggling with his pot belly. Of late he had put on weight, and his heaving was audible from a distance.

"Are you still around good people?" Dumbo shouted as he went into the library.

"Yeh still up and about in and around. Dumbo where thus coming from." Responded Daniel.

"We have made progress and it has been a life changing experience. People relate to us naturally, unlike when it's me in person."

"Daniel the only progress I can see is your skin, Mr President. Your skin looks great Daniel, you are shaven and shown, what's up with you two? Its' weird, though: seeing a brother, become so spruced up."

"Daniel, this is just getting bizarre no hairs look at your hands and fingers eel! Have you joined these clubs that scrub pluck and rub you over?" Dumbo came closer to look at Daniel.

"For me guys it's a no, no. I am a Kush man. I do not need someone scrubbing me and buffing me up, hell no; a brother keeps it real."

"My President you enjoy holidays better, without Maya. How can you glow like this, no trace of the cheeky moustache ohm? Caleb whatever you have done to this man it is becoming weird by the day."

"Shut up Dumbo, Kiki is waiting for you, look who is talking. You never got to tell me how plastic make-over, feels like." Daniel shouted back.

"Yeh cheerio don't you start with me, Daniel." They all laughed as Dumbo prepared to leave.

"Keep me posted. I am doing fine not many issues at the moment, parliament is on holiday, see you." Dumbo left with a question mark on his mind.

"These guys are not telling me everything. Are these guys undercover or under the sheets." Dumbo scratched his bald head.

Vice President Tom Dumbo was an easy going man. As long as he can do a little bit of work and ceremonial appearances he was a happy man. Food and women were his concern.

Dumbo relied on his private informers to keep him up to date on gossip. He somehow trusted his friend Daniel. He could not be bothered with rumours they knew each other well from Russia.

The Audit Report

The team of seven met at the Falcon hotel for a briefing and update of the audit. Caleb had already communicated with the team and was on the case. This time Daniel looked bright and alert; the red dress did compliment his skin tone. She had a matching handbag too.

Caleb passed on the chair to the audit manager. Josh Green was in his zone he worked as an internal auditor for 10 years mainly with quasi-government departments. He started working as an intern with the comptroller and auditor general department as a clerk. Worked his way through articles and the Institute of Internal Auditors. Later earned a degree in accounts and finished his Association of Chartered Certified Accountants, to supplement his accounting career. Josh was eager to debrief the team, knowing that the head of state is involved.

"We have done a mini-audit trail in the Ministry of Finance department. We checked the internal control systems and accounting systems. It does leave a lot to be desired, there is much to consider. Madam, as you may know, internal auditing may also involve conducting proactive fraud audits. This identifies potential fraudulent acts by taking part in fraud investigations."

"This way we can identify control breakdowns and ascertain financial loss."

"Mrs Soti, the reporting system is just so chaotic and bureaucratic.

There is a need for control limits in ledger accounts whether it's an adjustment or payments. Same should apply to cheque signatories, there is a need for an accounting control system."

"I have to send a fraud squad with your permission madam. Skamu approved payments to some women in his department and we have checked the years of experience. I have gone through the organisational structure, its fishy Mrs Soti. It is a lot of money over half a million and holidays abroad too." Josh had surely done his homework.

"Give me the report Josh I will deliberate with Caleb this is a serious matter."

Daniel was quick to put things into perspective he wanted to make sure that any action taken was not going to spill over and bring undesired results and attention from the wrong personnel.

Josh continued his feedback.

"Training is vital in most departments, they need a clear recruitment policy for all departments it must be a precondition. The bids on bilateral deals are questionable. It is a jungle out there."

"People are just surviving whether it hurts the next person or a friend, it does not matter. It's dog-eat-dog life."

"There have no work ethics and virtues because the leaders are just corrupt. It is now fashionable to be corrupt and the code language is (get down on it)."

"It is a passport to a chain reaction of mafia style. Mrs Soti you have been to the outlying areas. How is the rural population baulking under this economy." Josh wanted to make sure Mrs Soti is aware of the gravity of the audit.

"Josh I have cried since; see my eyes look puffed. Even Vice President Dumbo was surprised to see me like this."

You have contact with the vice president wow? It must be a major deal for you Mrs Soti." Josh's eyes said it all he realised how deep the audit was.

"Oh yeah, we had to go there with Caleb so that's how it happened." Josh just realised how much this work meant to his country.

One World Vision

The United Corporations headquarters is in Alaska. The military wing of the empire is the Red Nights. The Red Night's operations have a carrot and stick philosophy on its target nations. On the surface, United Corporations' focus is on African Development and political change. This applies to all the countries that are receiving aid. They also support African countries that align with their capitalist principles.

Start and Finish moved to HQ after the Kush victory when they managed to put Daniel into power. President Liberty Zorro had become a pain in United Corporations' back. His continued rhetoric never got any international media coverage and he ended as a lone voice in the wilderness. President Zorro had bitten more than he could chew. He went on a mission to nationalise many private enterprises including mines and diamond ventures.

The Daniel's road to power was a done deal, the Red Nights dominance system was working smoothly. The Kush electorate has no proper channels to question their leadership. They just accept what appears in their Television and radio sets.

The government officials were not a problem as United Corporation made sure the association structure was airtight with bribes galore. It enabled members to spy on one another.

Election manipulation was easy as the people rely on the media to vote and the corrupt leaders to follow.

Start and Finish got a hefty bonus for managing such a challenging portfolio. They sailed through without any uprisings or reprisals from the target nation.

Kush has large reserves of uranium and United Corporations was keeping an aerial surveillance on the goings-on in the country. With the oil shortages, United Corporation wanted to make sure the uranium deposit survey is ready for the nuclear energy demands in the next century.

Start and Finish became directors of operations, a crucial responsibility to manage the empire's division. Nothing goes unnoticed when a nation is under ideological change. United Corporation set up interests in many African countries which have mineral deposits. The investors come with the expertise to do oil explorations, diamonds and gold speculations. Many global brands set up companies in Kush.

Kushians bought matchstick, maize-meal, toothpaste, toothpicks, soap, tissues, and many food items all from these international based companies.

Surveillance

A contact friend of Start in Kush faxed a picture of Caleb and a woman, at a gathering in Chenga remote village in Kush. The United Corporation associate members spied on one another. The informer was a priest at a nearby mission school he surely smelt a rat.

"Can you fact find all the details of this meeting and get back to me" Start emailed the priest.

Start checked with the contact at Kush house. Daniel was on a working holiday and the wife was in Malaysia.

"Ohm something was not right this woman in the picture with Caleb looked like Sara Daniel's sister. Could it be Daniel's sister?" Start knew that Sara was a teacher at a private school or college.

"Ohm, interesting. Cannot trust Africans, this is ridiculous, no loyalty or a sense of purpose."

"Harvard training did not do much." Finish added.

"Whatever it is they are doing; it's not getting any media coverage. Why is it top secret? It has not gone through Parliament protocol. Argh." Start shared his frustrations.

The team were just settling into the operations division and merging their previous contacts. It was a slow process.

First and Finish needed to update the database to keep a tab on President Simba and his Adviser Caleb Biti. This package was a smooth operation, grooming Daniel and Caleb was an easy pursuit. They did not cause any trouble before. It was a too good to be true, life achievement, for these Kush boys finding themselves in America. Going abroad was an unbelievable stunt and the two had it easy but with a private cost to it.

****

President Tom Dumbo was settling into his role of acting president. It was a holiday season and parliament was also on a long summer break. President Tom Dumbo called his secretary Linda to his office.

"Linda sweetheart are you friends with Maya.

Come here Linda sit on my lap. Oh! Happy days,"

Tom was signalling Linda to come and sit on his lap. Linda just shooed him away with her file and carried on typing.

"Why Tom, what's up?" Linda tried to keep typing.

"Are they having marital problems, she has gone to Malaysia without Daniel they never are separate these two. It is the first time they have gone on different holidays since they got married?" Dumbo was grinning ear to ear.

"Tom it is hard to keep the fires burning, it's hard work to sustain a marriage. You are contemporaries you should be sympathetic. This is the time for shenanigans, so-called midlife crisis, and look at you the pot calling the kettle black. Tom, you are naughty you try to get it on the side, I will tell on you."

"Did you know that Caleb and I went to Mina Boys only mission school? I still remember a case where one of the priests was accused of some shenanigans with boys. Linda, you can pick a vibe among boys when something is going on. Unfortunately at my school I was the last to know. I was not a shining star or some smart Alec. They used to call me Dumb Dummy I loathed it, darling. I could sense something was going on but could not put my finger on it.

"Isaac was an altar boy I remember he used to go to Father Jacks house. Ohm... Linda he changed on me and became a bit reserved and scared. His grades changed he was one of our best mathematicians, but alas darling he just faded away."

"Isaac was senior to me and he stopped taking my groceries and started to wet the bed. The bravado and gung-ho was gone. I had one weakest link to laugh at, at least. Until the big guys were found out that they were harassing me. It was a ransom situation, just because my father was well-off."

"Talking of Caleb's father he was a police officer. One day he came brandishing a gun trying to shoot the priest. We did not get to know what happened to the head teacher."

"He was a disciplinarian and no one could dare challenge his authority so it was all hush. Caleb was taken out of the school to Mase mission where he met Daniel."

"Oh, Tom I did not realise you were bullied at school, I am so sorry. Here you are, now a President; let them stuff it down their sorry guts." Linda tried to console Tom.

"But you know something Linda; Caleb has never married and lives in a nice apartment in town. Very smart and some say he is a compulsive obsessive chap on hygiene issues. One of his colleagues says he scrubs his hands with a brush which he carries with him everywhere. He is a meticulous and Nicky, picky guy. He was always like that, some say especially when he left our school to Mase mission school."

"Ohm, so who is he kicking out with then?" Linda was puzzled.

"Linda, does he have any feelings at all? Such a handsome guy with everything a woman can scream for."

"Sir Tom, beware of skeletons in the cupboard." Linda tried to be cautious.

"But anyway what are you implying about this school kerfuffle. Was Caleb involved in the doodah? Maybe the dad freaked out and just took precautions being a man of the law."

"They say his father was a Sergeant Major in the Police force. Maybe he came and took his son from the school to avoid him being victimised by the system and the priests. Our school Linda relies on external donors and such a scandal could have hurt it badly, that's why it was hushed up."

"Our head teacher was a scaremongering madman, a law unto himself. He ruled the school with an iron fist and was a mister fix it. He was so protective of his position. Nothing evil could vex him as long as his behind was safe. He did not mind dishing out a cane on pupils behinds like Christmas presents."

"So darling I just share this with you, I know you are a private person. Caleb was not reshuffled from Daniel's cabinet since he took over. Caleb is a mystery to me I hope all is well in Jerusalem for him." Linda tried to get along with the boss's flow.

"But Sir you forget you were not reshuffled too, you are presumptuous and condescending. Where are they now, the two cronies we always call them" Linda asked.

"Ohm working holiday abroad and around, I hope all is well with those two." Dumbo looked excited and intrigued.

Salam Alikom

Daniel's skin treatments just made his skin glow as they travelled first-class to Dubai in the United Arab Emirates. Their first foreign trip abroad. Caleb could not keep his eyes of his President.

"Caleb! Stop ogling at me you making me feel uneasy."

"Come on man you now look like your sister Sara."

Caleb decided that they can do the makeover when they get abroad to avoid airport drama. He tried to think of every eventuality in case they bring attention to themselves. The airport staff did their usual routine checks while the two were safely ushered to the Very Important People (VIP), reception. The senior bag handler noticed that the bags were mixed up. Presidential luggage has a separate special scan area. The luggage handler could not believe his eyes. There was a makeup kit, female enhanced braziers, wigs, make-up, and silicone chicken fillets. It was mainly woman's clothes and shoes yet these government officials were just men.

"Guys we should not search these bags they are high-ranking officials. Maybe we have the wrong bags." One of the airport staff shouted.

"Diplomatic immunity guys, be careful. We do have some weird and awkward ones that come every day. It's clearly labelled for (VIP) Republic of Kush in Africa."

"Guys there is no harm done he has his other side, but they cannot practice it here its haram. It's a potential disaster for Dubai and Kush. Islam forbids such practice worse from a head of state."

"They have some men's clothes mixed with the boobies it's bizarre; it's haram guys. They cannot practice this in our hotels." The senior VIP check-in assistant whispered.

"Let them be. There must be a good reason or explanation for this drama. It might be a parcel for a relative. Guys, please write your memoirs and remember this day. You can make a load of bucks for this; don't say I did not tell you."

They all scurried to the checkout conveyor belt. The staff repacked the clothes and personally delivered to Caleb. Caleb sensed an unusually enthusiastic check out staff. They all smiled and fought over their luggage and Caleb just raised his hands in confusion. They escorted them to a limousine waiting in the reception concourse.

"Salam alikom" Mr President." Shouted Ahmed as he took his mobile out as if to make a call. He took a picture of the two cronies and saved for future use.

"Yeah, I do love my job," skipped Ahmed as he rushed back to his desk.

The Kush embassy is in an elegant, 50 storey building in the central United Arab Emirates, in Dubai. The climate was just pure magical, clean and beautiful people everywhere.

"The Middle East has beautiful women. They are the ones who cover themselves up, Caleb why is that." Daniel could not stop ogling at the girls that came to attend to them.

"I think there is dignity in this attire. In Kush, people are now so westernised and wear tight ill-fitting clothes with thongs and boobies hanging out. Man with trousers hanging down, showing underwear which was unseen in Kush."

Caleb made sure the clothes were suitable for the Arab country. Daniel wrapped up in a sari and headscarf, they headed for the embassy. Daniel wished he could have dressed like this all the time; it covered a multitude of sins. Daniel thought this outfit made him feel at ease to carry on with his undercover operation. The Kush ambassador's name was Cain he came to Dubai after Daniel came into power.

"Hello madam, welcome Caleb, you decided to pay us a visit, how kind." Daniel and Caleb moved to a deluxe conference room.

"So how is life and business around here? Daniel asked.

Cain was a confident man he tried his best to give value for money in his business engagements.

"Well, business is booming, bilateral deals are now slowly taking shape. This is a progressive country and we have interests in our diamonds and gas explorations. Saudi Arabians are shrewd business people, they have it all."

"They have man-made islands built to international specification. A world class city in the desert and Burj Khalifa is the tallest building in the world. It has 160 stories. I will take you there and see for yourself."

"The population is a mixture of Indians, Emirates, Pakistanis, Bangladesh and some young immigrants. They focus on the better life than their personal differences. Dubai is voted best place to live in the world. Life is good here, we have a few of our people in engineering, earning good salaries."

"The culture in many Arab countries has a lot to do with family values. I believe that any attempts to rid a people of their culture, it just destroys their individual fibre. Do you know that names have a bearing on who we are."

"A name is like a blueprint. Words have a spiritual impact. Therefore, we must be careful whose name we have. It's never too late to change the names we gave our children. Names should have meaning and heritage to bring good tidings."

"Arabs believe in beautiful ethics they call it, face. You have to earn it by family preservation, yet the world over it's the opposite. The world is now making efforts to destroy family and create lost tribes it's now the norm."

"It's all about family in this part of the Middle East. We all need a safety net when the world is unkind, with a family you can survive."

Cain took the two cronies out for lunch as pre-booked. Daniel was taking in the diverse array of colourful cuisines. Menus prepared right before their eyes; these were locals showcasing their culture.

He was at ease in his disguise and could sit comfortably eating a man's size portion.

"Madam you must be starving." Cain noticed Daniel's voracious appetite.

Caleb could only give Daniel the evil eye as he chewed his food.

"It's the jet lag, Cain, I have not eaten a thing for eight hours," Daniel retorted.

Cain was left in shock watching Daniel eat like a man, with big mouthfuls and quick gulps. He never met the President in person in Kush. When he got his appointment as ambassador, it was Vice President Dumbo who was acting President. Cain thought to himself that Mrs Soti was a woman who had not been well trained in etiquette and deportment. Cain kept wondering how she could eat man size portions. He kept the thoughts to himself, something was not in its place.

After lunch, Cain took them to central Dubai to check out the massive infrastructure and development taking place. The clean and organised functions of the city was a big contrast to his Kush.

"They have work ethics. From serving the family, you serve the nation; it's engrained in them. Many do not drink and when you are down the family takes care. They have minimal poverty in this country."

"Their religion I think encourages giving to their poor so it's progressive. I have lived here now say ten years, eventually you get to understand the people closer, than through the media."

"We have many religions in Kush and most are not by African inspiration they all started abroad. Madam, religion is an important element in any society if applied correctly."

"The Kush churches depend on the HQ international mother body for spiritual direction. This set-up is a typical structure of many of our churches. Kushians love going to church."

"Our attendance and tithe accounts records are in International Church Headquarters. Yet we are the poorest. In the West, they are closing down churches and not as religious, but they gave us the Bible."

"Religion is the philosophy and crux of our make-up. Therefore, it's been used, abused and controlled. Madam, our churches in Africa, are serving a bigger picture or interest of a global extent. We as a people do not realise that faith is an individual solo search, to do good, love and helping one another which defines God. Hence why anyone is able to bring their gods in Afri"

"There is a lot to manipulate in religion that's why it's the number one cause of strife because it's a catalyst. Religion touches people's innermost self, that's faith and conscience. It's a sensitive area susceptible to manipulation.

That's the area we Kushians need liberation through education. We can then all question everything than just accept whatever is written."

"A society should continue to discover the unknown. We must aim to reach the moon, under the oceans, in the sky; if education is the main drive. The unknown then becomes the known. Grandfather's tales can become cartoons, they are just fables and yes keep his invaluable wisdom."

"We are into this practice of visiting witch doctors and accusing this one and that one of causing misfortune. Why because of lack of light. Madam Kush needs more light."

"Enlightenment started when God created light, so men can see. Because of too much darkness in our rural areas because of no electricity. Snakes, insects' bites and night predators' hound the people. Kushians accuse one another because they cannot see what bit them. Kush is just crawling to civilisation we have a lot to do madam."

The pleasant and relaxed conversation with Cain gave Daniel a different perspective on life. It was worth the visit; if he had come as President, it is pomp and ceremony. Usually prepared speeches and protocol. He could not have come to all these places.

Cain took them on a tour of the Dubai shopping malls and the famous Burj Khalifa. The breath-taking designs and architecture blew him away.

Daniel wondered how Arabs could expand on desert soil and yet Kush has vast expanse of land and has little infrastructure.

"Caleb I think Dubai's success is based on their oil and gas riches. They can attract the best designers and business acumen. Their leaders are oil barons and the West comes in with all the expertise."

"We also have a lot of minerals and we should invest in Kush Mrs Soti, instead of depositing abroad. That is the money which is used to develop countries with stability like Dubai. Africa supplies the raw materials"

After a night's rest in a plush hotel Daniel was keen to take a break and see his wife in Malaysia. He missed them so much. The dazzling Dubai had given him rejuvenation and inspiration.

Central Intelligence Quotient

Finish was on his computer checking out the latest developments on Daniel Simba gate. He called another contact in Kush to fact find. Daniel was on a working holiday. His wife was in Malaysia alone.

"That is a first" Start voiced over Finish's shoulder. Weird people what are they are up to now. Never trust these Kush geeks, they change like chameleons. I hope they are not evading us."

"Sara, Daniel's sister, is away on holiday in the USA so it is weird for real. That woman is a replica of Sara but where is Daniel in all this. Who was with Caleb in Chenga Province? There is a woman dressed to kill, a city woman on a village visit. Usually, they dress in their African attire when visiting rural areas to fit in. It is common sense: Hey!"

"Start another email from contact Pee. He says the guys are in Dubai visiting the embassy but so far Caleb has been alone with the same woman dressed in a sari, same looks. Daniel entered the airport with Caleb."

"Get me the dossier on Caleb and I am still to make out this guy, since the incident at Mina mission."

"The priest got a transfer to another school. Intelligence says the boy was physically and emotionally violated."

"His dad wanted to blow the guts out of this guy. The priest was restrained and the school needs funding so it was hushed up. Caleb was transferred to another mission school where he met with Daniel. It's sad that in Africa justice can never be done, even on abuses committed by their own and worse by foreigners."

"The foreigners just buy the whole legal system. But something good happened later for which Caleb does not know of. The Church Headquarters heard of the scandal and quietly offered Caleb a scholarship to Harvard, he was a bright kid with a high IQ."

"Caleb soldiered through the trauma and from what I know the doctors have tried. From psychologists to therapists. He has a specialist Urologist in the United States. That is what they are working on and I don't think anything has changed as far as I know. He was in the United States three months ago so I don't think of anything with Daniel. Closet president; no I do not think so."

"They were just novice young and unassuming boys, thrust in a first world and they were focused. They do not drink and smoke."

"They did not party they were two innocent young boys eager to learn anything intellectual. They have the brains so what is this now. Daniel's kids are doing very well and he loves Maya everyone knows it. It could be a midlife crisis."

"Finish, maybe they became closer before we acted and now they are just trying to find ways to rekindle the fire since Harvard. Who knows? Caleb is smart maybe going to all these clinics and consultants is just a fuss to cover up his lifestyle."

"Start they have been together since High school they know each other too much. Too close for comfort. This can potentially become an African scandal of unprecedented proportions."

"You know that the Kush constitution is not amended and it's a no, no, no. It's taboo in Kush this can hurt Kushians. My gut feeling says wait and see, maybe its midlife crisis and Daniel wanted a break from his wife, to just go without Maya."

"Fair enough and Caleb might have finally started to seek ladies. Who is this woman, we still do not know?"

"That is the question" The friends just looked at each other intensely in unison.

****

In Kush, Vice President Dumbo carried on with his daily routine. The summer holidays were dragging on, and government officials were having a relaxed time.

"Linda, do come in please, I want you to fax this for me, it's the Chinese document." Vice President Dumbo was going through his tray.

"Hello boss what's up with you today."

"Close the door please, I do not want those no do-gooders to hear us."

"Linda…. Say I am now 65 years, is it too late to sit at the helm? You will be my adviser because I like you. You are a smart, well educated and an independent woman. How is that Linda, and of cause the extras that have come with you being my secretary. No strings attached."

"Dumbo get your beefy hands-off me. You are having a midlife crisis like your pal, Daniel. I am married and you have no say in my life. Ouch! You hurting me Dumbo, please stop!"

Dumbo was visibly seething.

"You do not ever; ever; speak to me like that again; I own you and I thought you knew better, understood!"

"Yes sir", Linda croaked.

"Good girl, now where was I. So what do you think of me as President Dumbo?"

"Sounds good to me" Linda tried to answer.

"If Daniel is not careful he will slip on a banana skin soon. He is like a kid looking for adventures, forgetting that he is a President. He is a good man, gone crazy, with childish pranks."

"Boss what do you mean what games is Daniel playing; are you not being too judgemental. He needs space why should he account for everything he does to everyone."

"He is the President everything he does Kushians should know, he is a public figure darling."

"Well everyone needs some solitude once in a while, give him the benefit of the doubt he is a good man."

"We shall see dear; am I forgiven, sorry for squeezing you so hard. I am a concerned person you should know me by now."

"Its' okay let me finish the filing."

"Sure darling." Dumbo looked dejected sensing Linda's mood.

Linda was upset and her hands had bruise marks. She went to the toilet and started sobbing. This was not the first time Dumbo was forcing her against the wall and groping her. His optimistic reveries, of becoming President of late; was just the right trigger. She had to go with his line of thought to keep her job and she loathed the other escapades that she has to endure.

A disturbed man, this Vice President she thought. Linda did not worry about President Daniel Simba.

She thought Daniel had picked up on Dumbo's delusions and was playing a mind game with him. Linda trusted Daniel, whatever it was she had no reason to suspect any wrongdoing. Maya's disposition was unpretentious; she could tell they loved each other dearly.

She had on many occasions met Maya at the presidential galas and official functions. They got on well Linda assumed.

Linda did not reveal to Dumbo that she was friendly with Sara the President's sister. She did not want him to start to use her, as a spy or something to further his dream of becoming president.

Family Time

Daniel was missing his wife, after Dubai he just wanted to be with her. Caleb managed to organise a stopover in Malaysia with the security details before he took off to the States. Maya was surprised when she got a call from Caleb, the President was joining her for lunch. She asked her assistant to cancel her appointments.

"Daniel, Darling you look ohm… Glowing what you have been doing, your skin honey is so soft. Bald does agree with you but this is super bald dear, no trace of hair even on your arms. Honey did you exfoliate, did you wax, hey! Daniel where have you been? Have you been on holiday; tell me where you went." Maya could not stop talking as Daniel got himself comfortable in a dressing gown.

"Calm down woman, what have you been drinking?" They sat on the beach loungers by the poolside.

"A man sometimes needs space you are a wise woman you should know this. I did travel to Dubai just checking out opportunities for the kids and other business interests' honey."

"We have to prepare I cannot be president forever. Dubai is da bomb it's another world in another time space dear. Beautiful people and vibrant culture. I ate like a horse, the infrastructure darling is just grand beyond belief."

Maya organised a spa treatment for them. They went in a sauna and sweated. After much drinking of water to hydrate, they went into the massage parlour. The two lovers lay comfortably on the long tables having their tense muscles worked on. The stone treatment was lush and Daniel was into it as the masseur moved in rhythm with his groaning.

Abel and Jude had their own arrangements; shopping and movies at a nearby posh mall. Daniel wanted to have a celebration surprise for Abel he had done well at Oxford. Jude was still an undergraduate. Maya organised a special evening dinner and a gift to keep the boys happy. These were moments Daniel could forget the cares of the world and just marvel at Maya and his sons. This was his world.

****

"Thanks honey for the surprise visit. I thought you had written me off as second-hand." Maya was chatting to Daniel in the drawing room."

"Darling you know that I am smitten with you. My life does not need all the Casanova antics taking place these days."

"Prime Ministers, Presidents being caught with young women and concubines. We leaders should be role models. The behaviour especially with political leaders; sanctions that it's okay sleeping with young women."

"When young people go on a rampage we are the first to blame them, darling. Power seems not enough these days, sexual conquest is part of the package. Maya I do not want to end up saying in court. I did not sleep with this woman."

"You funny Daniel and still got it, honey." They laughed.

"Some leaders have open extramarital affairs and do not care about the example they are setting for their people. Did you realise that in the bible the moment a kingdom failed to live an upright life and rejected God they somehow collapsed."

"The conundrum honey is lust. Man are in pursuit of fantasies. The most terrible effect is the abuse of children. That I cannot take. You abuse a child you worse than hell itself. Judge take the prison keys and throw away."

"Daniel, the crux of mankind's pursuit is lust, but now it's gone beyond reason. Man, resort to using drugs to go through the fantasies. Why because even the conscience cannot understand it. Love does not hurt. We adults cannot pursue fantasies of children, for me that's the end of civilisation."

"Lust is running the world, it's on every street corner. I used to cover my kid's eyes when sexually charged adverts appear on TV. The kids are traumatised. The question is who can stop this sexual revolution lest the children become very high-risk victims."

"Check throughout Bible history, leaders referred to the chief priest for directions. Nowadays whoever is the chief priest is rotten to the core. I suppose this puts the world in disarray."

"Who is the chief priest to consult, its all politics? If not politics its perfunctory religion, what people need is faith. We are too scared to take God at his word. Somehow we seek the charismatic orators to lead with empty words that signify nothing."

"This job needs dignity, stable family and everything else falls into place. All I can do then is to try."

"It's more about service than the power which makes this job exciting and above all ethics and virtues."

"Maya you never need to worry about a thing, I want to stick with you till the end. We started as friends and that says a lot. Thanks for the lovely dinner darling." Daniel stood up and gave Maya a light kiss.

"Abel is happy so there you are Dr Abel Simba our son, in the making, all by himself. Abel is prudent with his money and has a cool head. I have not heard of any shenanigans from abroad where young people get into drugs and clubbing culture."

"Many end up in jail, they do not mess around with immigrants, one strike you are in. American prisons are full of black people. In America it's like, it is the popular institution for blacks."

Maya was quick to remind Daniel of his own country,

"What about Kush, you detain people and imprison them without trial. What about presumed innocent until proven guilty. You use the same system to abuse your own race. Darling until we start to respect ourselves. The West will never deliver any anything better until we love ourselves."

The Mercenary

Caleb is a man of action he made sure he did not miss his important appointment in America, with one of his Urology specialists. He had to juggle between the President's undercover adventure and the usual administration duties. Caleb felt apprehensive he was hoping for a solution to his physical and medical condition.

As he sat on the plane to the States, Caleb was feeling the exhaustion from the tight itinerary. He kept dozing on and off. In the middle seat, a middle-aged white male wanted to engage in conversation.

"Are you a business leader or a rapper you well suited young man. I am Mr Kramer born and bred in Bongo."

"Nice to meet you. I am Caleb from Kush."

"I noticed when that flight attendant addressed you. She asked about you not being with President Simba. Are you part of his entourage? Sorry to be nosey. But hey we are all Africans."

"We do not thrive on gossip and secrecy" Caleb just nodded his head. He wanted to get some sleep.

"No, I am just a rapper. You got that right. I am travelling to see my friend in the States." Caleb had much on his mind.

"I spent three years in Kush in the 1990s. I wined and dined with the greats of Africa."

"I used to work for a big transnational funding group and we always come to rip you off."

"Your government put me into million dollar projects. Ventures that do not yield anything."

"Are you still with the group?" Caleb asked.

"I have since moved to yet another group with similar intentions. In the next few months, my colleagues and I will be in Kush to hypnotise the Lion King Simba. I work for a broker that has acquired a chunk of your debt. Your government owes not the World Bank, but us millions of dollars. We will be in Kush to offer your minister a couple of millions and fly back with a cheque twenty times greater."

"For real why are you destroying Kush with a carrot and stick policy,"

"You have no use of the money. If you have it, where do you invest? Not in Kush but abroad. Your equity is abroad, so I would rather the money be with those that can use it for their own kind." Mr Kramer could sense Caleb's fury and thrived on it.

"Are you aware that this plane, cars and many inventions are done by my people? All the luxury it's ours. What have you done in Kush that's typically yours?"

"Sir you are getting on my nerves. You are now insulting me." Caleb was now wide awake.

"Good I am glad I might be talking to a thinking head, awake and not drunk. You like the easy way out, without sleepless nights. When I go to the pubs, it's full of suited professionals drinking and wasting away. It's the same humdrum one day at a time 9-5 job."

"With us it's not golf only, we have working clubs where we share ideas, network and seek partnerships. You hate each other because of tribal affiliations, you cannot work together. I have to say our divide and rule works all the time."

"Listen, Mr Kramer, you should compare like with like. If I come and hold you at ransom in your house for 300 years, imagine the effects on the generations. That is if you even make it alive."

"Your comparisons are based on insincere, unjustified, presumptuous and condescending mentality."

"Your ancestors also came from a state of barbarism and developed into an empire. Allow Kush to go through the same process to find it's sanity in this chaos."

"You forget that we did live a sophisticated civilisation back then, this is a Roman civilisation time to reign."

"I am just helping you to move your civilisation a bit faster. After your drinking, all you think is women or which tribe this one is."

"You do not see opportunities you only see divisions in one another. You are lazy, slothful Kushians, dream big when you go to sleep."

"Now I am really getting angry. You just told me you have syphoned billions of dollars from Kush and you are happy about it. You are a sick man."

"Go on be reactive. I am glad, with all the dirt I see in Kush it has found a victim."

"The best creative people I know in Kush are the women. It's just ingenious the way women in Kush trade. Now they are in Dubai selling their doilies and wares. How they get there, only heaven knows."

"They set market stalls in every space they can find. To get money for kids to go to school. These women have to cook and clean at home."

"You young man should be there to make clean market stalls with sanitation facilities. Comply with the law and also do business in the process. This way you regulate and see that hygiene is maintained. It's up to you and down to your women folk they have much to do."

"Listen, Kramer, you should take your grandiose speeches to the corporations that employ you to corrupt us. If you know so much why not share with Africa in good faith."

"Do not divert the conversation son, I am talking about your amazing women. I have seen them in Mauritius despite the difficulty, they sell items. In Malaysia, they fly and sell wares door to door. That is the drive for success which needs to be infused into Kush."

"Through thick and thin they are able to sniff business opportunities. You, friend, are busy doing deals and corrupt practices. Why not ask your women how they make it in every country they go to do trading."

"I always wonder how these women who have no education are able to cross borders and do good deals. They have business acumen more than the people in your cabinet. You take short cuts with the nation's coffers. If you say NO, we won't force the deal down your throats."

"You lot you sing rap and busy cussing your woman. Words are powerful you can not expect divine blessings when you insulting the womb that birthed the nation. Words are us, words are life."

"Even in the good book, God says there are blessings and cursing in words. Do not curse the women you are supposed to protect. We have honoured our women and treasured them as the weak and precious vessels. That's civilisation."

"There you said you actually partake of the corruption. You provide the means and the avenue. Mr it's you who creates the cycle of corruption to a hungry nation." Caleb was seething.

"You have a lot to learn from your poor people. Moonlight and find better methods to achieve a task. Having initiative is okay.

When you have clubs, have an opportunity to just share information and partnerships than just entertainment. These clubs can create communities within communities."

"It's okay sometimes to research and do it for self-growth without expecting money or funding. The rewards will come later. You are too lazy to think. That dirt and grime on streets which is seen as normal can be big business."

"Kushians can set up a garbage collecting services. Why wait for your government to do so. Charge toilet facilities and provide the service. Charge for hiring tractors and combine harvesters to farmers."

"Simple service. You want to wait for us to do it. You want us to come and clean that litter strewn everywhere for you."

"Okay, sir I hear you. The environment has to be enabling to have that impetus. It's a lot to unlearn to be able to achieve that vision."

"Yes, it starts with you, young man. Use that money from rapping and help your Engineers build something to help in kitchens. Small inventions that can make work light in the field. You rejoice doing very laborious hard labour and it's the woman doing the grafting."

"Instead of quaffing and drinking, please have time to sit and plan. Find solutions in your own communities." Mr Kramer looked satisfied with himself as he dozed off to sleep.

Caleb was seething with rage and failed to get a wink. The culmination of events was just prophetic. The journey they have decided to undertake was making a structure of itself, it brought in revelations and insights into Kush politics. Caleb pinched himself imagining how his President had agreed to such a risky exercise. Kush has its fair share of International Relations critics and such a move Caleb thought was just unreal.

He chuckled to himself thinking about how Daniel thought it could only happen in the movies. His President had managed to go through the process without acting lessons.

Caleb carried with him his strange conversation with Mr Kramer, the Caucasian passenger on his flight to the USA.

****

"Good to see you, Doctor." Caleb sat on the chair next to the Doctor's table.

"How have you been since the last operation, any signs of action?"

"Slight sir: just minor movements."

"Undress, lie down then I have a look." The doctor directed Caleb.

Caleb connected a flight from Dubai to the States to meet his Doctor. He had a small operation to correct some nerve damage inflicted when he was still in High school by a priest. Doctor Morrison is a specialist Urologist, keen to get Caleb well again.

"Ohm seems it's going to take time to heal; it's a slow process. Keep on with the exercise and keep fit. Go have another X-ray taken then we can advance to stage two of nerve repair."

Caleb hoped that one day his health problem should improve. He wanted to be able to blot out the trauma and start a new life. He had to rush tomorrow and meet a close friend on holiday in the States.

He scurried to Malaysia to prepare the next trip to bring President Daniel Simba to the UK.

Confused Intelligence

"Zee what's up with Daniel where he is now?" Finish was on the phone talking to his contact.

"With His wife in Malaysia" Zee answered.

"What about Caleb"? He should be with him I heard.

"What!" Finish shouted.

"Yes you heard me; they are in Malaysia enjoying the spa and all. The son did well at Oxford. I heard they were having a special dinner party in his honour.

"Ohm; okay, old man I will talk to you soon" Finish banged the phone.

"This puts all our theories to nothing, he is with his wife, its false intelligence. Why should we worry then about the mysterious woman with Caleb when Daniel is canoodling with his wife right now? They were naïve and focused and now play cat and mouse with us."

"Its holiday time and Daniel may have wanted a quiet time away from media focus. He might have just asked Caleb to do the work. He might have avoided media attention, to just relax and be normal.

He was with Caleb at the Dubai airport so it's him in person with Caleb and suddenly this other Kush woman appears." Start interjected, Finish.

"No harm has been done. There is nothing untoward in the media in Kush so let him be. Caleb and Daniel are not out of the woods yet. I have some dossiers to work on in Bongo. We need to increase surveillance on the two cronies and give a proper feedback to Top Dog."

The Diaspora Awakening

With airport entry procedures done and luggage processed, Caleb and President Daniel waited patiently in the Heathrow VIP lounge.

"Enjoy your holiday Mr President." One of the check-out managers bid Daniel.

Caleb and Daniel were taken to the Hiltons, a luxury hotel in London.

Caleb prepared an interesting itinerary for the day. He had in mind a mixed grill of experience with various Kush and other African immigrants. Daniel saw an opportunity to get to know what goes on in the Diaspora. He read mostly news from Kush pro-government media.

Daniel used to come to UK to shop at Harrods with Maya, amid high-security details. Sometimes they have dinner with the Queen and never visited the estates. The official visits become pomp and ceremony when he comes to the UK. Daniel could not fit in a timetable to have a meeting with the Kush immigrants. The demographics of Kush immigrants lived mainly in London, Lester, Luton Manchester and Birmingham.

It always started with one family member and the rest flocked to a place where there is a friend or family. Many immigrants found menial work. Each has a different story to tell but apprehensive of the future, and some still toiling trying to get a semblance of normal life.

"Daniel your embassy this time will be your people, ordinary Kushians. Your people are surviving in an environment; where they are not welcome but get protection from the law. Some still strive to survive and making it despite not getting benefits. Especially those that are still illegal."

Daniel dressed in a casual long linen skirt and a pullover top. With a long summer cardigan, they were all set to go on a round robin trip in the UK. A family in Hounslow in London was their first visit. Caleb knew them from Kush; they were friends of his cousin. They lived in a shared occupancy in a rundown area of Meadow estate. Caleb arranged with them to come see how they were doing and introduced Daniel as his cousin. The family of four was all crammed into two small rooms and shared the three-bed house with another family.

"Well, this is it, England for you. We have been in the country for five years and no valid immigration papers. We have applied for asylum and were rejected, we are saving money to appeal. The lawyers are expensive they charge by the hour and it's getting so dear."

"What are your reasons for an appeal or asylum claim?" Daniel asked.

"The economic situation back home madam. Life is hard in Kush we exist like wild animals no one gets to know how they fend except the creator."

"No matter how hard you work in Kush it's not enough, the government wants a pound of flesh."

"The international banks do not give us loans they are tight conditions which we cannot meet. It's a catch-22 situation and we follow the money here, it's better here, we are economic refugees."

"But why asylum Mr Kondi," Daniel asked.

"Here even in my situation my kids can go to school and the most important thing is food. We never are short of food. At least it keeps the body and soul alive."

"I do cleaning and my wife is a care worker, so it keeps us going. London is beautiful do not be fooled by our house. It's the cheapest we could afford, if we get our papers then I know we will buy a house somewhere." Mr Kondi was becoming animated.

"But you did not answer my question why asylum?" Daniel was insistent.

"We are not from Europe so the only route besides education is seeking asylum. If one is a European, you can travel and stay anywhere in Europe. They take care of one another. It's us the non-European immigrants that are in trouble, we are outsiders. We are the undesirables."

"In Africa we put barriers and visas to block one another out, we belong nowhere. I am willing madam to surrender my citizenship and just live to enjoy peace, no wars, and no tribal squabbles."

"The leaders in Kush preach and breathe tribes. They are so divisive it fuels hatred among Kushians, it's pathetic. People get into power and they have no inkling about service. No clue about the enormous load they have to carry to channel their people to better vision."

"This should be the base of my power if I were president. Seeing my people and my country getting healthier with better services."

"It's sickening madam when we become full of knowledge and no ethics. Leaders go and look for human solutions in theories and calculations when the solution should be within us. Compassion, care, love, empathy, sympathy, patience and wisdom. This has not come to our leaders."

"Why do they go on platforms and talk western philosophy and feel so pompous and full of themselves. They do not think much about their people."

"Leadership is not about an Oxford qualification. It's about what one can do to make the lives of people better and finding solutions to problems. We are sick of hearing excuse after excuse ma'am,"

"They all cry Oh it was because of socialism that's why, next oh it was because of capitalism."

"There is something wrong ma'am, with Kush leadership and everything right with its wonderful trusting people."

"All the people need is bona fide leadership. Tell the people the truth and be open. No matter how much the West can meddle in our affairs."

"The first point is to deal with greed and corruption. It's a disease that will disenfranchise Kush and slowly recolonise it'self. Greed and corruption are a recipe for colonisation. Top government guys deal with international foreign investors and most deals are eventually for personal gain."

Daniel could only look down and sweat in his pullover.

You Caleb go and advise that Harvard geek boy Daniel, you work for him. He is just so crafty and seems not to care about us. Hence, this mass exodus of Kushians. Tell him to shut that department of information. It's just a propaganda government mouthpiece, he should be talking to the people like President Zorro did."

"Zorro tried, bless him. He was constricted like that snake does, the boa constrictor. The big guns shut him up and shipped him to the grave."

"Why, because he wanted the masses to wake up and build communities. Any African policy that benefits the ordinary people is counterproductive to the big guys. They need to benefit from us and control our destiny."

"It's us, the illegal people and the children that are seen on TV poverty adverts who are the result of Kush's mala fide leadership."

"That Daniel should be ashamed of himself a good-for-nothing learned buffoon."

"What is this education for; when it's used in Kush for evil to suppress the people; it's a travesty. Caleb, my friend, go tell Daniel that what goes up will surely come down. The change will come but at a premium price. Check in the next century we might not recognise our native land."

As the head of the house spoke, he was passionate and obviously well-spoken. Daniel was disturbed by this man, a simple cleaner. He left Kush where he was a physics teacher. It was a reality check that his own people are willing to give up on a distinguished and life enriching careers. They come and clean toilets. Daniel looked at Mr Kondi with respect and confusion.

"People realise there is more to life than just the Kushian poverty stories circulated in media. Kushians are capable if given the opportunities to progress. Immigrant's hurdle is the race barrier which is a challenge and the new society we now live in."

"But honestly I would rather miss the beautiful Kush. From being a teacher of physics in Kush; now I clean toilets in the UK."

"Oh Madam our men have been humbled, my wife is a care worker. She tells me that Kush men are also working in care jobs. You know how patriarchal our family structure is."

"It's a humbling journey seeing man from Kush cleaning and working in care homes. Some had never washed their own clothes, this is a rude awakening."

They all laughed though Daniel was sweating under his pullover.

"Some were directors of companies and university lecturers. In the UK, they are more like nannies. Tell Daniel he needs to know that people can change because culture is dynamic. We need to start talking this message and walking the messages too."

"We are not primitive it's the leadership that has ransomed us and our wealth. Please tell the President that we need good governance and best practice throughout the country."

"Then people will come back, many have a lot to share and the focus is not on amassing wealth anymore. We want to share our best by helping the poor that's how this country does it."

"Madam, here in England no one cares what you are doing. You are just a number as you try to make a living. In the UK, we are just another brick in the wall."

"Go to Victoria station, sit and watch how people move about. They are focusing on where they are going not on the other person."

"In Kush it's always someone meddling with someone's business. We must look to nature maybe we can start to be inventive than resote to tribal and personal attacks on each other."

"In UK many things work, trains, buses, roads, and work rules are standard, that's civilisation, madam. Someone here is doing their job somewhere and everyone is working on the same goal, unlike you Caleb."

"You are sitting on your fat backs thinking of deals. When a politician takes an oath to serve it's not for his family, but for the whole country. The vision is to look for solutions for the greater Kush, not his family."

The kids came from school they were smart, happy and well adjusted to UK life, despite their immigration status. Daniel realised that even in their difficulties this family had decent clothes, shelter and food a basic human need.

Daniel and Caleb bade farewell after a lovely brunch of fried steak, cornmeal, and green vegetables in peanut butter. It tasted just as Daniel's mum made it at home in Kush. They snacked on roasted peanuts.

"You do not miss the home diet you seem well covered," Daniel noted.

"London is a melting pot ma'am." The head of the house said proudly with his apron on.

He was able to cook and serve without feeling odd. The wife was still grafting a long day shift from 9 am to 9 pm. Diaspora changed the Kush man.

Daniel did not change his baby's diapers, he did not know much about the kitchen. His mother, sisters, wife and workers do everything for him.

As they prepared to go to the next assignment, Daniel found the diaspora inspiring. He looked at Caleb and said.

"How come the best cooks are men? In the West and Middle Eastern cultures, they are master chefs."

"Is that all you grasped my wife, you only could look at men all these trips. Divorce is coming wifey. I am the man you cannot behave this way. I will tell the clan back home that you have wondering eyes; men can cook Oh!"

The two cronies laughed as they sat on the high-speed train to Birmingham.

****

Caleb and Daniel arrived in Birmingham the second largest capital city in England. With enough hours to spare, Caleb took his President on a tour of the city. A city that is as diverse as the rainbow. Daniel could not help commenting on the aura and spirit of this massive city. A melting pot of colour and races.

After a meal at a quiet restaurant, Daniel was thrilled that he is able to mix and mingle than being taken to posh places. This was a real deal visit, not perfunctory Presidential travels.

"Caleb I have seen Asians, Jamaicans a mix and mingle of African races. I have seen the Caucasians mix and mingle its business as usual."

"I am amazed, this typifies diversity at it's best. In Kush, we cannot get along with people who look the same. Imagine that in the UK these cultures hurdles of language, religion and culture."

"That is why I brought you for a drive incognito. This way you are not detached. Power takes leaders to a position where they become cocooned. Distanced from reality with a multitude of mouths to speak, work and do things for them. It's a numbing position and it goes with the territory. Daniel, it's best to find time to reconnect."

"This is the dilemma of our time. Ruling Kingdoms that separate people by class, religion, culture and race. The opposite way is not accepted because it has socialist overtones."

"Education becomes the only way to liberate the people so that they can liberate themselves."

****

Birmingham meeting was in The Glitz 5-star Hotel in a conference hall. Caleb organised with his contacts to get immigrants from Africa and Kushians to come and brainstorm.

An "**Africa Agenda, Africa's Future**," was the topic for discussion.

The secret service ensured there were no cameras and everyone was asked to switch off their mobiles and leave them at the entrance in special lockable bags.

University students, intellectuals and business people attended.

Caleb used the Kush embassy to do the invites including marketing, hiring, refreshments and eats. Caleb introduced Daniel as his partner and no one took an interest.

Kushians were itching to put their views across to this government aid.

The conference tables were set up in clusters. People could sit and move, but still in view of the podium. Waiters could easily walk around and take orders. Buffet tables were lined at the back of the conference. The delegates walk in, choose, pick a plate, snack and napkins then sit at the earmarked tables. The atmosphere was relaxed as people chatted and snacked before the programme started. Caleb gave an insight into the situation at home. Stressing to the audience that Kush needs its people to come back to jump-start the economy. One young woman bolted and shouted.

"That is all you can say; jump-start. My days! Why don't the lot of you jump-start with the loot you get from African government coffers."

Applause was deafening Kenyans, Zambians, Somalis all started to shout the same message. Daniel rose and screamed for everyone to keep order. After a while, Daniel (Mrs Soti) told everyone to be calm.

"You are all frustrated and it's understandable. Someone has to take a stand and take the first step."

An elderly woman rose and said,

"To jump-start what you have ruined with the help of your foreign friends; where the money is you loot, it's in Swiss accounts. Not even in an African country?"

"You come here to ask for the little money we work for, to feed our families. You cannot feed them you come here in your smart Harrods attire. Why did you not shop at Next it's cheaper."

One old guy stood up and mumbled.

"Thank you madam and gentleman; for taking the time to feed us all and to have a forum to just talk. Here in the UK we are all sucked up into our local politics. In England, they work day and night."

"If a Member of Parliament messes up in the UK, surely heads will roll. In Kush if a Cabinet Minister messes up they get a promotion."

"Can you two cronies, sorry madam go around this country and sit with local governments authorities. Go and see how hard they work. How committed they are, it's a nerve centre. A sewage bursts in Kush, it's no big deal. Here you get sacked possibly the whole department."

"The system works and the corruption is minimal. We see the benefits to the poor; not the rich people only. I am not saying there is no corruption but at least they have the decency to attend to the poor."

"The local authorities in this country work madam, so go back home change your Gucci shoes. Put on working clothes and know what is meant by grafting."

"Good work comes in dirty overalls ma'am. Government ministers walk freely among the people they cycle to work and you waste our money buying Porsche cars. Why do you need an army of security personnel, what are you afraid of? Hey, the guilty are afraid."

After the meeting, Daniel was complaining of a pounding headache. Caleb gave Daniel some Paracetamol. They thanked everyone then mingled briefly with the crowd.

A young woman came to Daniel and told him that in Kush she was a housekeeper. She was now a qualified nurse earning enough to feed her whole family. She had bought a new car and travels abroad on holidays.

"Some of the migrants have beautiful houses furnished to a high spec with fine art and décor. They grab whatever opportunity comes with both hands and fly with it. They are living the good life." The young woman looked radiant, confident and well dressed.

After the Hotel meeting, Daniel and Caleb dined at the professor's house. Daniel saw that his people have a good life. The professor lived in a big house on a private country estate.

It has four garages and a small field for a horse and a pony. Daniel saw the opportunities of such good decent living. The aura was different from the usual Kush moan and groan introduction to this is my life.

Daniel had seen many like him and black celebrities always linked to a poverty background.

"Why is life so hard for Kushians? I am part of these people's future story too." Daniel reflected.

What he had seen at the professor's house was a different story for the next generation. They played on the piano and read poetry. Daniel saw that at least among all this political chaos; Kushians fought the systems and defied all odds.

"If they can be successful here, why should Kush be so undesirable?" Daniel pondered.

Daniel found inspiration in his people the Kushians. How can we leaders be so insensitive to the plight of our people? Each man for himself and God for us all." Daniel remembered someone saying this.

****

Caleb took Daniel to Bath and Wells in Somerset England. He wanted to show Daniel some ancient baths used by the Romans. As they went on a tour of the museum in Bath, curators were well informed and able to answer every question. The tour took them through the history of the Victorians. The books Pride and Prejudice, Sense and Sensibility, came to life at The Jane Austen Centre.

The artefacts and simulated events of this British culture were portrayed with fine artistry. After a cup of tea and cake, Caleb drove Daniel to Wells.

"Daniel, tea was once a treasure, it was gold. Did you hear what that curator said, they used to reuse teabags a lot? See how far mankind has come from. Now we throw it like rubbish. There is hope for Kush, my friend. Our enlightenment will come."

As Caleb drove through the British countryside, Daniel was amazed at how accessible and easy the villages were. The countryside was even more alluring and picturesque than towns and cities. Civilisation had allowed the citizens to work together to build communities and retain peace. The countryside well planned and amenities structured to meet the needs of the villagers.

They walked around the Bishop's palace and sat down to have some tea in the café. The structure of the castle is well preserved and maintained to keep the history of the British Empire. As they circled the Bishop's palace gardens, Daniel was attracted by a Sculptor.

A Cross with children barely able to carry it. Some of the kids were under it and still trying to hold on to the cross.

The museum curator explained the meaning of the sculptor.

"It represents the way in which the world's children will have to carry the burdens of their parents' decisions and activities.

Disease, Aids, hunger, landmines, and homelessness, lack of education, war and poverty can all be seen in the children, who carry the cross of Christ. The work is by Josefina de Vasconcellos (d 2005)."

On the sculptor, it was written,

'The Weight of our Sins.'

"At this moment as they stop for breath before staggering on with the burden of the cross, we are given an opportunity to relate to this group of neglected children."

Daniel went and sat on the bench just opposite the sculptor.

"This message is I see in my dream. The words are exactly as I see the kids. Emaciated, pain filled tears and dirty. Oh my....It's just as my dream puts it. We the adults are creating their world and it's full of pain."

"Daniel I think you are getting paranoid. We are in England and you talking of your dreams in Kush. What is the correlation here?"

"Caleb the case for the children versus adults is a worldwide petition. I see sexually abused kids, poor and sick children in my dream. We the leaders have a major role to play, to protect our children."

"The problem is that I have this dream regularly. I do not want to start on tranquilisers to have a deep sleep. It's the same kids and same faces but they are multitudes of them pushing and shoving. I am trying to find the meaning. What chance was there that I will come to Wells from Kush and revisit my dream on a sculptor? From Kush, Caleb, think about it."

"I told Dumbo that this undercover operation is a spiritual quest of finding myself and my humanity. Here I am, going full circle. This journey we started has a great awakening. Thank you, Caleb. From it being a trivial pursuit, I am totally overwhelmed."

"President Simba this journey has indeed been a spiritual rival and enlightenment. I had no idea that this dream was still recurring. You need to create a conducive environment for Kush. The children deserve better. You complain about the adverts so now is time to make sure no Kush child is an advert for poverty. Let's go back to London and prepare for Kush."

The Golden Professor

Caleb could not contain his excitement.
When they came back from England, he received
a letter from Professor Small. Professor Small
taught Caleb and Daniel at Harvard in the USA.
Professor was inviting himself to Kush after
completing his round robin trip to Gambia where
he was tracing his ancestry. President Simba asked
Daniel to organise a special tour in Kush for
Professor Small. He made contacts with
Universities for special appearances. The media
was set on alert to pre-empt a visit from a great
man who propelled the leaders of present day
Kush.

"I am over the moon, we never thought of
checking on good old Professor Small. I thought
he had passed on. He is say 85 years and still
looking for enlightenment. I am in awe of this
great man of wisdom. He made our study more
enjoyable. Coming to Kush is historical." Daniel
could not wait to meet his hero and mentor.

After a hectic schedule from one appearance
to another, President Simba wanted the professor
all to himself. Professor Small was taken to the
most beautiful safari camp and game reserves in
Kush.

Despite the harsh conditions caused by the poor economy, Kushians were jubilant. Professor Small was shown by Kushians their natural aura of humility and genuine welcome.

Professor broke down at one point as he walked in the market square of Edom city, seeing how happy the people were. They hugged and even told him to come home for good. This hit professor Small at the core of his heart. He cried that he indeed he was home. He was jubilant that yes the Kush soil is home. The Ministry of Agriculture was ready to give him a piece of land if he was ready to settle in his motherland. Professor felt more energised as he smelt the air and ambience of his people. The birthplace and continent of his great, great, grandparents. It was an aha__ moment for Professor Small; to be connected to students, he taught in the USA and now leaders of a progressive Kush. He thought at least he can now rest knowing that his little contribution to opening the minds of his people had led to a President of Kush.

Daniel wanted some quality time with Professor Small to reminisce and delve into the deep end of civilisation. He awaited his rational perspective on the state of the nation of Kush. As they sat on the veranda with an array of eats specially made for Professor Small. The two great man enjoyed the sunset.

"Education is the most powerful weapon of mass enlightenment. This was said by Nelson Mandela, Daniel." Professor sat comfortably on a couch with special cushions to support his spine.

"This is the reason why education was deprived during slavery and during colonisation. It is indeed a weapon of mass enlightenment."

"If more Kushians become educated they will leave the dark practices and use the weapon of the mind to liberate ourselves."

"Education is the only way to reason with a fellow human or else its fables and fear factor. I see the way tribal divisions in Kush and cultural differences makes ruling Kush a tall order. I feel for you, Daniel."

"Professor I am very humbled that you took time out of your spiritual journey to find self and come to your other soil, Kush. For Caleb and me, it's a moment of truth. We could not have sailed through at Harvard if it was not for your personal devotion. We seek your wisdom to solve this problem called Kush."

"Yes, it's a lost voice in the wilderness to rule during this present Kingdom. You are not a sovereignty, you are part of an international community. Your generation is now equipped with revelations. The internet and social media avenues will awaken the conscience of the people."

"The issue I have is this; If Africa is not on the motherboard of inventions. Africa will become virtually subservient, it's going to be worse than the real slavery of our time."

"Get your young people to train in science and technology. Give sponsorship to increase information technology or else virtual slavery is coming. Game of dominance is at the door."

"It needs funding Professor, and yes opportunity cost has to apply but a Kush budget cannot give allowance for future benefit. It's short term aggrandisement fiscal planning and yes very ready for recolonization."

"Son I do not envy your position. You are a juggler with diverse, business, political, critical, spiritual, unethical, tribal, international, secrecy and Kush juggles to throw."

"How you keep your head on I have no idea. It must feel lonesome at the top. As long as you have a place to empty your anxieties and concerns you will survive."

"The dilemma then comes... You cannot save God and Mammon, you must choose Daniel. The quiet place you go to alone is ruled by the two. God promises peace that surpasses all understanding and Mammon promises hell on earth. God promises eternity and the other the abyss. Choose."

"In the quietness of nature find him, in the stillness of the air feel him. In the heat of the day embrace him and yes nature and science explains him completely. Do not ever, ever, lose the peace."

"You have this life to live, all it asks is for you to do your best. The evil that will be presented to you is meant to strengthen you to seek positive reinforcement."

"The power of Kingdoms is in armoury and land, you need to keep your country safe. Security is the word or else someone is going to mishmash the security for you. Do you have intelligence of who is who in Kush?"

"You won't know who your enemy is after they have reorganised your borders."

"Thank you, Sir, I am honoured to be your student. Never thought in a million years; I could sit with you in Kushland it's surreal."

"I am indeed overwhelmed by the greatness of your country and the love of my people. I have met a people full of humility and no malice. Content and hoping for a better tomorrow."

"They are waiting on you the leaders to make a change. The change is held up by a force that is greater than Africa and it's still prevailing. Better hurry with change before poverty and hardships sears the people's minds. A hungry man is an angry man."

"It needs a bulldozer of mind and soul intervention, to remove this grip. It will take human sacrifice, lots of sacrifices to get to a promised position. God is still in control."

"Son without a free mind and education in Kush. It's going to take divine providence to remove the scourge of the reign of this ruling Kingdom. Sad to say it sounds defeatist."

Professor Small was so enthralled by Kush he invited his family to come and see this part of their inheritance. The people of his continent. President Daniel Simba could not have it any other way.

He wanted the Professor to make Kush one of his homes away from home. Investments from the USA started coming in and African Americans wanted to be part of Kush and bring business.

A small book called, "**Living above the Law**" by Professor Small and inspired by Kush professionals was now available in Kush bookshelves. Briefly it read

"The healing of the nations will come from a fruit of the soul diet. A science plus nature equals understanding God. Africa's revival will come from a position of deep, soul-searching. It's a top-down approach.

The good book laid it out with qualities and traits to rise from the depth of despair.

Joy…is a nature that we must enshrine in our being and as a nation. A pursuit of happiness and good life is through hard work. Let's make hard work pay. Laughter is the best medicine it's said. A people that can laugh at themselves are able to be critical of themselves without being overly sensitive. It is worth the effort to check the happiness of a country, the reasons why not are the reasons why we are in power. Everyone wants to come to a happy home and in turn a peaceful nation.

Seriousness does not mean business. It does take a lot of good governing, to come to this position or else its fake joy based on fear and an ignorant electorate. Joy is interdependent on the other traits.

Longsuffering… is a nature that we need, to allow forgiveness, and give each other second chances. A long suffering heart is not stupidity but wisdom and giving each other the benefit of the doubt and a desire to undestand.

Gentleness…Let's create a nation of people that are not brazen, loud, cussing and impatient of one another. We need people that will be gentle with their female folk, treasure and love them. Gentle people can gently love their nature and also learn from nature it without harshly destroying it.

Gentleness does not reflect weakness but a person who is patient and takes the time to handle issues. It takes a strong heart to be gentle and a hard heart to be cruel.

Goodness....is synonymous with virtues, integrity, excellence, principles dignity, and ethics. These are the traits a nation should enshrine in their declaration of governance. With all the elements of goodness, corruption will be put in check, vileness will be in check and only good-will can prevail. There is longevity in goodness because evil has crushed many empires. Goodness will bring forth exemplary leadership and not rogues and chicanery.

In schools at universities enshrine these ethos, not bravado and loudness and cussing. We have a lot to learn from Japan and other Asian countries how discipline has catapulted these nations to first world status. It's the use of the mind and seeking the goodness of their country in nature. Nature holds secrets to our survival.

Faith.... The substance of things hoped for and evidence of things not seen, so the good book says. We have no gods on earth but only one supreme God. We are on this earth together as humans no one better than the other. A deliberate direct, bold approach to God is the most liberating achievement. Empowering one another that there is direct communication with God. Let's remove the hurdles that we construct and empower the people that they are fearfully and wonderfully made. Therefore, we are each other's keeper. The duty of man is to worship God without all the drama. Focus on science and nature to understand God's master design.

Patience...Synonymous with forbearance, tolerance, restraint, stoicism, fortitude, sufferance, to endure. This is a trait that has brought about the many inventions we now take for granted. The man on the moon. In space, they stay in awkward and intense, unusual conditions for months on end. People have taken risks to find good land throughout the world.

It was through patience that people can move to an unknown land and settle.

Patience is a virtue that we need to build in our young people for them to have the patience to toothpick and create great inventions. This is an attitude that has to forgo noise, loudness and rough situations.

Let's work to create a nation of calm patient people and instil this quality in ourselves to appreciate science and technology. Hard drum beats and the hypnotising sounds are only to sensitise for a little while. Inventions take time.

Therefore, we need to create a calm and serene space for our children. Restraint and self-restraint are a virtue that calls for self-examination. With patience, we can evaluate and see better options. Restraint is a virtue that leaders need to have.

Temperance…Synonymous with teetotalism, abstinence, abstention and sobriety. This a direct call to a nation. Slothful drinkers will only get slothful decisions. Running a country is sacred and only calls for people that are ready to sacrifice their self and person to rule multitudes. A pursuit of excellence and love for humanity. A position that calls for meditation and self-reflection, therefore, sobriety keeps the mind in check with reality. A leader needs a clear unpolluted mind to have vision. Money is not the drive but power to give the greater good a pleasant stay on this temporary sojourn on earth.

A deliberate approach to train the young generation to make them driven and personal growth targets through national service and intensive science and technology programmes will bring forth results. Invest for future benefits.

Peace... Synonymous with calm, calmness, quiet, hush, silence, stillness, still. A panacea for human survival. There is a need to seek peace with self and in turn this can filter to a wide audience. Peace starts within an individual. Kush will prosper if we seek mediation and non-conflict resolution methods, not war. Soft power is the most progressive thinking ideology for the survival of this Kingdom. Peace is also about seeking it. It can only be found in quiet, still, noiseless spaces. A very particular connection to the soul with the omniscient. A secret place where the finite connect with the infinite. A pursuit of peace requires a surrender of the hustle and bustle of busy lives.

A nation must create spaces for its people to go to and unwind. It's usually found in nature. There a thorough appreciation is a requisite to connecting with the creator. Peace is a catalyst for happiness.

Love... Love is the answer to all our ills. Love encompasses the all virtues. It is doable to live above the law, but this needs a corporate, national top-down approach. The pursuit of excellence and cleanliness is the pursuit of the good life for all Africans.

Without detesting dirt and grime, excellence is not achievable. Patience, stillness, perseverance will bring about the qualities which can only be revealed to a people that seek peace stillness and quietness.

Architecture, mysteries of science and medicine, secrets of nature are revealed to those that seek that space. Let's have our children raised in peaceful homes. Places where they can thrive with positive reinforcement.

This is a promise we can give to our future which is our children. Why because our children's lives matter.

Confidence…..a mental attitude of trusting in self a person or thing. A virtue parents ask to be instilled in their children at school and institutions. It is the confidence of self that can transcend active energy to others. Through positive reinforcement and giving each other second chances confidence is built. Patience is a requisite recipe as our children learn new skills and ventures.

This is time to spare the road or else you spoil the progress. As it requires a healthy state of mind, it means that it should be cultural practice to speak good and not evil or negative about others. This needs a culture change to become a nation that looks out for one another's good. The curse of the people's tribe 'FEAR' needs serious and voluntary programmes to unchain the shackles ensnared on the people.

From witchcraft to negativity it's fuelled by fear. Subjugation is from fear. Sports and adventures to train our kids can mentally prepare our kids to have confidence. Fear is a scourge that put us in slavery, bondage and poverty. Confidence can replace fear.

****

Philosophers and great thinkers in Africa gathered at a secluded private Hotel in the countryside. President Simba worked with Professor Small to benefit from his wealth of knowledge and his natural intrinsic connection to Africa.

The Hotel was within a beautiful lake and safari park. The men and women came with a vision to present to Africa a change of thinking. A vision to change the weak points and strengthen the strong points. SWOT analysis of Africa's philosophy on life.

During his stay Professor Small communicated with his counterparts in America to brainstorm with professionals in Africa with Kush as the base centre. The response was overwhelming and some Americans wanted to find avenues to participate in the business expansion.

Each country was represented with funds pouring in from American businesses and African philanthropists.

President Daniel Simba and Caleb met with the Kush technocrats and philosophers.

The great think tanks carefully selected by an academic council. This idea came about after marathon sessions between American philanthropists, educationists, and philosophers from around Africa. Professor Small had the privilege to attend all the meetings and share his expertise. These were game changers seeking enlightenment and not self-glorification. A group charged to create a vision and deliberately trained to change the Kush governance scenario.

The team produced a Kush Indigenous Report on Corporate Governance.

Issues covered were;

Corruption

Fear factor

Good governance

National Security

Pursuit of happiness & good life

Corporate social responsibility

Best practice

Culture

Excellence

Patriotism

Ethics & Virtues

Science & Technology/Engineering/

Food security

Health & wellbeing

Children's vision

Virtual transparent fiscal management

Intelligence Leaks

Start and Finish had increased surveillance on Caleb and Daniel. They sat in the office with Top Dog Bob. He only came around if there was trouble brewing.

"I told you to keep a close eye on these two cronies we have a lot of interest in that country. I am not ready for any stupid tribal and military coup intervention. Our mines and plantations and businesses do not need this climate the two cronies are about to create in Kush. We had this in the bag from day one and you got your reward."

"Mobo, the Defence Minister, is not a happy bunny, he is almost getting out of hand. He has been doing his own clandestine activities sabotaging Simba in areas where he has no support. He sent the green bombers those young people to massacre the whole village. He is a law to himself and not playing by our rules. We did not realise that he is a relation to Zorro, so he is a dangerous character. We need to deal with him too."

Bob was not happy he was visibly angry.

"To add insult to injury, Skamu the scammer you know him, he is the Kush Finance Minister was moaning to our investment team about undercover audits. He said Daniel gave the orders, he was cheesed off for real.

Skamu treats our people well and the young women from his office are good fun."

"Kushian ebony queens they entertain our staff at home and abroad. Skamu approved our venture and these private auditors found out; about ten million. Skamu is one of us. I cannot allow Daniel to lay him off we need his stupid spending head to get our deals through."

"My bosses were happy with this project. They have not heard any riots for the past 10 years. What was Daniel thinking? Why did he have to keep it a secret and no media? That's the way we can intervene properly." Bob looked at the pictures and laughed so hard, the office echoed.

"Where are they now"?

"In Kush, they intend to fly to Havilah on their United League meeting.

"Good, get the plane and itinerary details, you know the standard elimination package. I have use of these photos a lot of uses for plan B. Get me Dumbo's dossier I do not trust that other Kush top military guy Mobo he is too excitable and eager. I want a smooth transition. "We use, abuse and throw way."

****

"Linda: are you ready to be the first female adviser to President Tom Dumbo in the Republic of Kush darling?

"Oh there we go again, are you in your happy mood today Tom?"

"Oh! Linda victory is now certain.

Let us wait and see my dear secretary and you do not sound enthusiastic honey why?"

"Let me be the cautious one. I let you dream on Mr President we have to complement one another. It is a secretary's secret pact." Linda quipped.

"Ohm sounds good to me darling." Dumbo came closer to Linda

"Well, what do you know: the two have been banging one another all along? Going here there everywhere working holiday Argh!! Wrong; it's skeletons in the cupboards."

"What are you talking about Tom?" Well, I am reliably told that they were caught out in the act?

"What!" Linda looked shocked

"Pics and videos, hugs and smooches Linda." No smoke without fire darling, what did I tell you."

"Dumbo you know how easy it is to be snitched and pictures superimposed to make them look real."

"Not this time honey, this is first-class world news not even on Kush channels."

"Oh, that even makes it unbelievable. They are the real scammers the Western media. They can do anything to get their breaking news. When they want you, they can get you. They even kill your lot, to get their lost teddy bear. So honey, do not believe anything you hear or see." Linda was clearly not excited by the news.

"Not this time. Linda listen to your boss I have my lead as well. It all clicked in the end. Linda my contacts worked it out, and our suspicions were dead right."

"Local or abroad," Linda asked.

"Both Linda, trust me. I keep my enemies close and play dumb. I was not called Dumb Dummy for nothing in High school.

Moment of Actualisation

President Daniel Simba and Caleb sat in the basement and chatted about their escapades around the globe. Daniel was now wiser and seemed eager to make changes. The audit team had done the final reports and did not have to travel abroad. The audit team was working their socks off, amid the resistance from the departments.

Ministry departments were hesitant to provide information to the audit team. Josh Green sought Caleb's help to get the information needed to carry out the audit.

"Caleb I have no idea where to start, where to go and what to do. Pay the auditors from my allowance. This experience was so real; not some media conjured story. Follow upon on Tina and chase up on that kid Isaiah and make sure Ministry of Mines sees that these miners have the proper equipment. We do not want another Chile mine disaster.

"There will be no TV cameras in Kush to see if they are alive. That kid needs to stop working, he should get a full-time education and prepare a scholarship for him. He is the next generation worth saving. I want that boy in University. The parents need help with medication as well. Let's help them to get back on their feet and look after the children."

"Did you manage to connect with Ron? Do we need to wait until I have the briefing with the Health Minister? Antiretroviral drugs should be available to everyone for free."

"All the money that's wasted in deals should be used to get these drugs and condoms as well."

"Caleb I know that we force hospitals to collect money. We must have respect for a grieving pregnant mother. This I cannot fathom its barbarism. Let us do something for that woman and provide for her new-born baby. Charge the burial costs from my personal fund. The social welfare department should be involved as well to settle her."

The whole undercover adventure usurped Daniel's energy levels.

"Caleb the holidays are over we will have Parliament opening next week. Let's sit down and compile the auditor's findings and write a report with facts and figures. They will not know what hit them. Skamu the Finance Minister; that Casanova might soon be looking for another job. The local authority heads need to attend this meeting. Caleb I mean business I am sick and tired of protocols that do not bring results.

"Take it easy Daniel, Start and Finish and the whole crew will take you down.

"Caleb, I told you I am living the end of my life so what the heck, let them finish I am started."

"Ohm Daniel you are a changed men, you need to take time to reflect."

"Caleb one last thing, you have been writing my autobiography, please include everything and write truthfully the guise and all."

"Send the manuscript to Sara's publishing house include current details. Caleb, we can always update when we come back. This way the proof-reader can start on the project."

"Do not worry, I am updating every time on my laptop. Sara will have direct access to the file so she will have the latest. We need Sara to put a high secrecy seal on the book until we leave office. Sara will edit and publish. The printing press is at the farm, no one can even fiddle."

"Caleb this is important, write a separate letter to Sara. Just in case anything happens to me she needs to know the Swiss number. She must take all the money in that particular account that account from United Corporations."

"All the funds are to be used for gifted kids, managed by Sara and Maya. It's for all Kushian's rural kids identified by school heads and Sara knows about the school project. No kid to appear on TV advert before we do something."

"I will write a prologue for the book I will give it to you tomorrow. Include it in the book but Sara must see all this when she edits. I hope you did justice to the person you are Caleb."

"Well just the usual, what we did together from village to Kush house."

"Caleb have I told you how much I love Maya.

I could not have settled for less she just completes me." Daniel rarely was this open about his feelings.

"I have learnt a lot from you, Daniel, you are a good simple, humble, honest man. After this adventure, I cannot see you failing to do anything."

"Do not forget you are the first President to go undercover and to top it up, in a woman's dress. That is a first-class act, Mr President. A Kushian, how taboo can it get."

"I am so glad Caleb you are my friend, my pal, my confidante. We did manage to just be adventurous. We did not have this opportunity in the time of our youth. Remember Caleb the good book says. Enjoy the days of your youth."

"We could not afford to be silly; our head teacher was a scaremongering whip man. At Harvard, we had no chance to be us. We just presented what we were there to do; education."

"Daniel you have taken a position any man can freak out to do. A President for that matter and you never failed. Come wigs or clumsy handbags you were just brilliant."

"Caleb, it's what we can do, with what we know now which will determine the success."

After the trip from the USA Caleb was anxious to talk to Daniel about his extraordinary meeting with Mr Kramer. Caleb had no clue about the deal Mr Kramer was referring to and which ministry it pertained to. After his morning business meetings, Caleb approached Daniel.

"I met this white man Mr Kramer. He thought I was a rapper and started talking about him being a consultant for a global transnational company."

"I just played along with his rantings, he thought I was a rapper. He said that he is coming to Kush to hypnotise you to complete a multi-billion dollar deal."

"What, who is Kramer and whom did he talk to, which ministry? He might have just used my name without an idea of whom he was dealing with."

"Oh my Caleb, there we go again, another corruption gravy train wreck. Does it ever stop? The system is so awash with corruption it's now fashionable to be corrupt."

"You would know if I had anyone at Kush House for any bilateral deals. There is no smoke without fire. Why was he so keen to empty such confidential information?"

"He thought I am a rapper with no inkling of business. He had a lot to say, some very valid points about the African continent. I listened and he talked a lot, he had facts to support himself."

"Well, corruption is a worm that is crippling our continent. Ignorance is a very expensive commodity."

"When these ministers see the investors from overseas they drool and have no inkling about business terms all it takes is just a hotel booking and palm greasing, wham bam water projects are gone."

"Sometimes people spread all these stories to give us a bad name. Caleb how do we deal with a problem like **Corruption**."

I am Healed

"Doc there is movement and I have been having you know those dreams."

"Oh, you mean every boy's nightmare." Doc interrupted,

"Yep."

"This is good I am excited for you Caleb I can feel some flow, the veins are visible and pulsating. Caleb this is incredible, what a turnaround."

"The new consultant was cautious on your second operation. He thought you had defaulted to zero. Now we need you to do something, the nurse will tell you. She will give you a cup and put the stuff in here. I want a sperm count."

"Oh yippee, that's more like it Doctor." Caleb could not contain himself."

"Easy tiger count your chicks when they are hatched. Oh, excuse me Caleb, no pun intended."

"Sure doc can't help it." Caleb took the little cup. "Well, that is a welcome bonus Doc."

"You look okay and much elated, have you been to see the psychologist at all."

"I have been so busy with the president. I had taken my mind off worrying about it. The president's assignment needed me to be 100% alert. It was a challenging and difficult exercise, doctor."

"Caleb the results will be ready today and all the best, Caleb you deserve the best."

"Thanks, Doctor. I need to rush home my woman was waiting for this news for 10 years. It's a long journey home Doctor."

"Come, here son give me a hug you are one brand of a man. And few of you, these days." Doctor had developed a soft spot for this soft-spoken Kush man.

****

Caleb could not wait to get home to tell Sara. The flight back home was taking too long. The Undercover sting did help to put his mind off worrying about the healing process.

"Did you tell Daniel?" Sara asked Caleb

"Oh no!!, Sara I was so scared to tell him. Most of the time I just doodle and gaze at him. He looks so much like you Sara and he is the President."

"When you get to read the manuscript you will understand what I had to go through. I have seen you through him. I am glad I am marrying into a wonderful family. I am a single child so I am safe now.

Sara looked radiant."

"I love you, Caleb, I have waited for you all my life. You were nervous that last time at the clinic in the States but it's worth the wait." Sara held Caleb's hand.

"I am glad you been at my side all along. I love kids and I could not ask for much. Just a healthy baby that's all."

"Caleb; wisdom does come softly. Our patience and the willingness to forgive and let go and let God be; has lifted the burden and healed you. The mind has to come in and take control to reverse the negative thoughts that constitute the trauma."

"Well, here we are, come close Sara." Caleb knelt on the hard veranda floor.

"Sara I am asking for your hand in marriage."

"Oh wow it's an engagement ring its beautiful Caleb, I do care for you and Yes I do; Yippee!" Sara was ecstatic.

Caleb lifted Sara through the patio door into the living room.

"You got to do it right, ask Daniel and then go see my parents you know our culture. I will take you to Aunty next week. They can arrange with Daniel and family. You know the protocol it's got to be done." Sara was busy kissing her lovely ring.

"Tell me something Caleb. Maya has been laughing at Daniel. She says his skin has been glowing and well-kept since you started the working holiday assignment. Did you notice any changes with Daniel because Maya keeps ranting about it?"

"Do not mind those two lovers, Maya and Daniel are two love birds" Caleb tried to avoid the question.

"Our Aunty in the village called at the farm. She spoke to mum that a man and a daughter that looked like me came to the village.

Aunty told mum she seriously looked like me. I think Aunty has seen you with Daniel before, so who were you with?"

"It was an internal auditor overseeing the assignment." Caleb thought the old woman might have found the truth.

"She says she felt connected with that woman. Aunty is weird you will meet her again she is the eldest and oversees any marriage in the family. But oh boy she can speak and jabber, jabber for the whole of Kush." Sara laughed thinking how her aunt can be comic.

"I like her she is the best Aunty anyone can ever have." Caleb was quick to respond.

"I am glad you had a chance to meet her or else you could easily have run a mile. Our cousin's boyfriend was so intimidated by Aunty. He just bolted out of the hut and did a runner. Bless him; she says she can feel something about people. As she said this story, guess what? It turned out that cousin's boyfriend was a fake, he wanted to just marry into money and skeet.

He had no job, dressed up every day to go and pickpocket at the market. She has a gift that Aunty to suss people out."

"Wow she is good", Caleb retorted.

Presidential Address

Traffic came to a standstill as President Daniel Simba came to open the 4th session of the 7th parliament of Kush. Security details were sprawling everywhere amid tight security. It was a nightmare to get into Central Business District (CBD) for travellers and motorists alike. Kushians dropping off or parking their cars on the outskirts of the city found it impossible.

The lockdown of Zorro Avenue to make way for Simba's style procession caused a traffic nightmare in Edom City. The morning rush clogged all roads in the CBD. Security was trying it's best to direct traffic at major intersections.

"What is all this palaver, is the day of salvation before us? They have blocked us out, and we must be going to hell today. The better part of the city is a virtual no-go area just because the President has come to town. It's not fair," said a disgruntled cyclist.

Kushians that came to work on this day were subjected to a thorough search. Kushians were so used to being abused and handled roughly by the security details nothing was new. The only struggle was keeping alive and getting to work and back home safely.

"This is what happens when the big cahoots come to town? The whole country stands still it is ridiculous. Hope they do not want our tax today." Shouted an old man on his scooter.

Chauffeur-driven in a Rolls-Royce, President Simba made his way to the House of Parliament. It was a huge procession which included police officers on horseback. The latest top of the range cars were on parade. He discouraged Maya from coming advising that it was going to be a tiring process.

President Simba amid the pomp and ceremony inspected a guard of honour mounted by soldiers from the Presidential Guard. They were sweating after standing in the sun, on duty since early hours. Police on horseback, donning a 100-year old colonial uniform, escorted the President.

Kush's top military brass were there to receive the President. He was looking fresh and resplendent in a grey suit and a white chequered shirt. The moustache was back and the long planning had returned his skin texture. Simba put his left hand over his heart and sang the national anthem at attention as 4 jets flew past, followed by a gun salute. President Simba then inspected the smartly dressed soldiers before retreating into Parliament.

After President Simba had entered the House of Assembly, Chief Justice and his contingent of Supreme Court justices came after.

They followed closely behind clad in the red colonial gowns and off-white wigs called toupees – worn by barristers in Commonwealth countries. Military generals followed closely behind.

The usually buoyant President Simba did not respond to his jubilant supporters' praises and chants. Simba wanted to get down to the business of the day. President Simba wanted to say his mind and was keen to finish the proceedings quickly.

The State opening was attended by heads of government, legislators, ministers and diplomats. Giant televisions screens televised the Parliament proceedings in every city in Kush. It was full coverage of Simba's speech.

It is business as usual as Kush parliament opens, it's usually ceremonial type, boring protocol of long winding speeches. Grumblings in the House of Parliament covered the august house. Vice President Dumbo was jovial than ever and happy chirpy with all the ministers. Daniel did not want to mince words.

"I welcome you to this opening of the 4th session of the 7th Parliament of Kush. Without further ado, I want to go against protocol today. I ask every minister to read the copies handed to them. I cannot follow archaic systems and protocols when people shouting outside expect us to better their lives. I am tired of us seeing them sacrificing in silence and hoping against hope that things will change."

"I am sick of the gun salute. I am so sick of the horses forced to canter and honour me when a child out there is hungry. I am so sick of all this hullabaloo ceremony as if I have died.

I am not coming to a dead parliament am I? I am sick of all this jet fly past when kids are hungry. I am sick of this regalia that has no bearing on Kush and what we should and can do."

"I am sick of everything and proud of every Kushian that has respected this office. Kushians have hoped against hope that things will change. Kushians revere us as leaders and we continue to take the mickey and take them all for a drive to live in hell."

"President Simba asked Caleb to print out a report on each ministry detailing the internal control shortfalls and recommendations. The whole house went silent as they opened to their department pages. Gasps and moans came from Skamu the Finance Minister and the Agriculture Minister Zumba could be heard."

"I will give you 14 days to respond to this report and I need recommendations on the way forward. We have no control and the subordinates have no control. This parliament is a Muppet show, no reality, no humans in the scene. This has to change I do not care whether you have other bosses that you swear allegiance to. The bucks stop with me. The people out there need our help they don't need your power or authority.

Kush needs your presence, reassurance and action. If you cannot have answers for them, then get the hell out of parliament and go back to selling peanuts. That's what most of us are only good at."

"We are the people that are allowing slavery to persist. We have shoved our people to go and fend for themselves abroad. They are creative, even in harsh conditions. Why, because we the people in this house are crap. We can only develop if we think outside the box. If you just think of your tummy and no one's, then you are an animal. Go scavenge because most probably you are scamming money from the government.

We need to stop this corruption now!!!! If you feel like dealing, go on the stock market be a dealer and deal with bulls and bears, not Kush money that's the taxpayer's money." Daniel bellowed to his cabinet."

"What have you done to make your country proud?"

"A lot of young people are just waiting for us to do the right things to make their lives better. Let me know as well if you are still willing to serve Kush, not your pockets. No tribe, no partisan politics anymore in these chambers and house. We are all Kushians with different languages. We can learn from each other's strength and become a unique country. The whole continent needs one universal language as well. It's easy to start with the young and they learn fast. You adults are the most divisive people, you tell the child about tribal differences. Hello, we look the same. They go overseas and they are worse off because racism started at home. I am this tribe and that tribe yuck! How about Hello I am Kushian and I am proud."

"I honour the mothers of this nation they have tarried with us Kush man. While we are busy killing our own generations. They watch and tarry as we make wrong decisions and find comfort in other women. They watch while we fail to give our children 100% effort for the sake of the next generation.

Women have tarried with us as we breed hate and violence. Using guns and machetes to butcher and harm our own flesh and kind. We use and abuse kids for our enjoyment.

The point is gentlemen if there is no hope for us the man, the head of this nation. Maybe let the women come forward and do it. We have abrogated our responsibilities and thought of short-term enjoyment at the expense of sacrifice and legacies. The Kush woman looks for food. She dresses the children looks for water and shelter. The Kush woman is pregnant, with a bunch of wood on her head, a bucket of water on the other hand. While she holds another child on the other hand.

Guess who is on the back.__ It's the man. We then proudly say 'The Home is the Woman.' Yes, but who should be the provider? __'The Man'. Not runaway dad. How sad is such a picture? I know many men are doing the right things.

They are few and fighting a losing battle to become the X and Y chromosome of Kush civilisation. Man was bestowed with both ribs of the human genome the X and Y factor. Great, husbands and professionals out there.

But hey the statistics are coming home to roost in our country by its state of affairs. Should we men all take a sidestep and continue our wanton lifestyle. Should we at least let, the women take over. We cannot offer anything better, we too stuck-up in greed and hatred."

"Gentleman and ladies we have a choice to make, either you are with me or we part ways today. We have to start somewhere. Let's put our house in order and cover each other's nakedness. Then we can face the world with one voice."

"Our children are crying and waiting for us adults to create a safe and clean environment. The abuse, harm and poverty of our children is a scourge that is coming to haunt us all. Children's lives matter. The change has to start with us. Change we need and change, we can. Aristotle has this to say about a state."

"Every state is a community of some kind, and every community is set up with a view to some good. For humankind always act to obtain that which they think is good. But, if communities aim at some good. The state or political community, which is the highest of all. Which embraces the rest, aims at good in a greater degree than any other, and at the highest good."

Organisation Of Africa

The African heads of state meetings were held in a private hotel on the outskirts of the city of Havilah. They went through their usual protocol and information sharing. The cultural exchange programme with poets and dancers in colourful clothes performed for the heads of state. Daniel felt tired and spent. The speeches were the usual solidarity rhetoric. Caleb always complained to Daniel about the lack of vision and action plans to harness Africa resources for Africans.

Not much was discussed at these gatherings. The professionals wanted to hear more about challenges to the effective participation in science and technology. The once larger than life man sat slumped in his chair looking lost and sullen. The hellos, how do you do my brother, how the missus and goodbye is was all said. Caleb tried as much as he could to cheer Daniel up, his spirits were low.

After the banquet, Daniel was ready to go home as planned.

Caleb set aside some time on the plane back home to ask Daniel for Sara's hand in marriage. As they came to the end of the meeting. Caleb wanted to make sure that Daniel knew his plans before the new parliament season. Caleb chuckled realising how suave he had been and Daniel never smelt a rat.

"Mr President you have been unusually quiet you did not say much at the meeting."

"Well what can I say, the chair is now with Bongo I did not have much input." All Daniel wanted to do was to talk with his mother and father on the flight home.

"How is my favourite lady, I love you, mama." Daniel finally connected with difficulty to a poor network party line on the farm. They found it difficult to use the mobile phones.

"What is the matter Daniel, are you okay son, where are you?"

"Its' noisy mama, just a little turbulence can you hear me? I am coming home mum I am on a flight to Kush from Ghana."

"You know dad's hearing is bad; so talk to me, Daniel. Maya is home so you should be happy, after the hard work you been doing. Well, done son, Abel has done well at University, another Doctor in the making. Daniel; Eh! Aunty told me about Caleb asking Sara's hand in marriage."

"Oh mum, you have cheered me up. Caleb is here, right here with me. He is a smooth operator, he was hush all along."

"See mum that's why I felt the urge to talk to you. The family is growing mama. I will skin him alive, Mr smooth criminal before he even touches my sis."

"He did not show any signs or tell me. I work with him every day. Oh, I am so happy mama…Oh no mama something is gone wrong mama; mama oh."

"Daniel what's going on Dani…eel? Answer me. Hey." The phone shrieked and went dead.

The news was all over Kush networks. President Daniel Simba's plane caught in turbulence and wing caught fire. No hope of survivors. Personal Adviser in the jet with President. The only information was from the international media.

"President Daniel Simba's Jet and his crew are all missing. Air traffic control failed to pick any signals; location still unverified.

Kush delayed sending reporters to the suspected area where the jet had been spotted. The whole nation was waiting for closure. Kushians knew about President Daniel Simba's powerful speech and his threats to sack government ministers. Rumours were rife that many Ministers are in line for demotion and possible job queue. This was the most exciting news for Kushians they compared it to President Zorro's cabinet outbursts and sacking of lazy Ministers.

A president not mincing his words and just saying it as it is was unheard-of in Kush. Daniel did not care about the dangers of his actions. The reports were leaked to the press and international media. Intelligence was informed of possible protests planned in the major capital cities. This event united a country that was once divided by tribal lines.

Every TV channel and political commenters spoke in unison. They were convinced that Simba was a man of mature politics who loved his country. The elders in the city also praised him for standing up for the greater good. Kushians believed it was espionage antics and another Zorro debacle.

For the first time, parties were now rallying behind this late President. Honouring him for standing up for the truth and sacrificing himself. For once the Kushians were talking about Kush and not partisan politics. They sing about Kush and the Promised Land they stand on. Kushians talk about the wealth and riches they have. The beauty of their country and the diversity of their people. Kushians now want a constitution for Kush by Kushians and used by Kushians.

Businesses became apprehensive worrying about loss of business. International buyers were edgy about Kush. Local Businesses acted quickly, advertising their goodwill by giving foods to schools and children's homes.

The Members of Parliament pledged a mass movement to get every serving officer to commit so that they can be held accountable. The whole nation was ready to sacrifice and get every voter to vote and have a say in politics.

Kushians now want those that are knowledgeable to create an informed electoral process. With one voice, Kushians are now sure that their views can be heard and actualised. They all want a basic needs approach where communities can only be set up after shelter, water and food are within reach.

Kushians want to pursue the good life and happiness with hard work, more land use, food, water and bigger homes for their families.

Botched Conspiracy

"How come you did not know about the Parliament opening in Kush? Bob was huffing and puffing, up and about as if in a trance. He went to the bar and smashed the glasses to the floor. Went to the fishbowl and was almost crushing it when Finish came from behind and took the bowl. First and Finish held Bob and shoved him on the couch until he calmed down.

"Bob this is the first meeting after the holidays it is procedural." First was unaffected.

"It's the usual Kush's hullabaloo they do this every time, it's just protocol."

"Not this time boys, Daniel has a report about schemes and scum in his cabinet. It also connects our guys, some having fun with office stuff from Skamu's office. Here read this." Bob dropped a detailed memo on the desk.

"You have all lost your steam. You might have been Start and Finish now you are *caput! Finito!*"

"Daniel is dead after you have allowed this undercover detective to uncover all this. I am gobsmacked."

"Our association system works and of all people you allowed these two clever cronies to bit you to the game and lose their life. We could have gone to plan B. To preserve life and threaten with the doctored pictures." Bob was pacing up and down and visibly angry.

"You are fools, there are lots of stories in these pictures. Caleb not married and going around like a Mr and Mr. Now it can never hold water and Dumbo is not steady. Skamu is too trivial. Mobo is too volatile. We need a clever but susceptible block who won't know what hit him, that's the plan." Bob scratched his head and sat down.

"Mobo the defence douchebag is too serious. He breaks the code by openly offending his rival Daniel, and shooting and looting in villages. He is too angry he wanted his cousin to take over after Zorro. He is a Rottweiler he is no good."

"Let's act quickly before the dust settles. Okay let's do it this way, Dumbo out, lets' puts Skamu in. We will have to do damage control and get the guy who did the audit to be the finance minister."

"At least he deserves some recognition. We need to silence him he did a thorough job. From organisational structure to control limits and so forth."

"The guy is seriously legitimate and a professional auditor."

"Do not foul up this time guys. Keep Dumbo guessing he is no good. Our informer says he abuses his secretary. I cannot deal with this man-mad-mess. Let him act as President before the next elections and the rest is history we are back in business."

"Protect our investments and interests then all will be honkey-dory. Nuclear is the next energy source and we cannot afford to be messed about. Skamu, our man, will deliver the goods lock, stock and barrel."

Bob was the top guy and always found solutions for their global empire. United Corporations and The Red Nights division.

Mixed Emotions

"What!! Are you sure you are pregnant; you never told me anything, Sara." Maya looked in shock at Sara.

"I know; some issues in life are better left unsaid until the time is right. Caleb went to the States for his check up. The Consultant Urologist gave the all-clear."

"It's not been an easy journey for him. Caleb is a determined person, between work and tight deadlines. He squeezed his appointments thousands of miles away. He never revealed his pain." Sara wiped her trickling tears.

Maya and Sara escaped to the countryside away from the hustle and bustle of city life. The nation's sorrow overwhelmed them and solitude in the country was a way to find peace. The two women cried helplessly. The birds joined in their sorrow twitting and chirping in the background. The cows, sheep, goats and chickens did not want to be left out. With a moo; moo here, a bah, bah there, here a quack, quack and a twit; twit. The whole countryside was sincerely ushering in a new dawn on Kush. The Kush blazing sun did not want to be outdone. It was sparkling and shining to keep the hopes and dreams of a better future alive. The gentle breeze at sunset just slowly rested the weary souls from their toils and cares.

"Sara Oh Sara. How, why this way?" Maya lamented.

"Life can have strange turns, Maya. No matter how clever we think we are there is nature to remind us there is someone in charge from above. A sovereign God, who has given us choices. Given us domain over all species, given us freedom for he says."

"Whom, I have set free in the mind, is free indeed."

"It's the mind my sister-in-law; that's where all conjuring of evil and good happens."

"As a man thinks so is he."

"It's true Sara we need to work on the junk in our minds to free ourselves' sis. I miss Daniel he was a wonderful husband and friend. The kids cannot be consoled. He was more a friend than a dad. How they quizzed him when he decided to work over the holidays."

"I know Maya, I was complaining to Caleb too. We have not been on holiday together for a long time. His doctor complained."

"It was all emergency appointments."

The sun was gently receding into the horizon with flickers of orange and gold flames. Maya touched Sara's belly and felt a kick.

"Oh, there we go, a Caleb trying to come out into this world."

United Corporations sent in extra help to keep the peace. Kushians were in shock; the drama in parliament awakened their souls and their being. President Daniel Simba's actions in Parliament went viral on YouTube and other media networks.

He had finally seen the true colours of his cabinet. Kushians wrote to the media and Facebook.

Some kids were heard singing about their ministers.

"What have you done for me lately, Hooooo.... yeh."

Kushians felt they never gained a relief from poverty even after gaining independence. This time, they could have a Kush spring, uprising. Kushians felt they had nothing to lose, they never had anything good from the government. Daniel's rhetoric had given them a voice.

They could now tell off the big airheads and pot-bellied Kush cabinet ministers. The women and children poor, scantily dressed were sure they can tell Kush government to shape up or ship out. They wanted the Kush government to work for them and not for family and friends only.

Kushians were fed up of egomaniacs, with an inflated bravado, no humility or humbleness. The women had seen enough of wars, tribal disputes, hunger, and poverty. Women are asking to be given a chance at the helm if their men are finding it hard to protect them and provide. Women are determined that they can do a better job.

The children ask for food, water, clothes and shelter from mothers. Our women are fed up with egos of a few men who are turning Kush into a dead zone.

Revelation

Dumbo was now acting President and jovial about it.

"Told you so!" He quipped to Linda with a cocky laugh.

"Come on boss, you are just an interim President, we are going to have elections soon then we shall see. Be cautious like me boss don't count your chickens until they are fully hatched."

"There!" … Dumbo kept slapping his pot belly.

"I am fully hatched darling. Come over here. And..."

"Don't you ever touch me. If you ever, ever touch me again, I will go to the press. I will reveal all your covert actions. I have then on tape. Secretly stored, with a witness to confirm if anything ever happens to me Dumbo. Get your beefy hands off me sit down Humpty-Dumpty, stupid man. No wonder the country is in trouble you think with your____."

"Okay that's enough now, get back to work Mrs Personal Adviser" Dumbo was livid.

"Good!" Linda smoothed her hair and cleared her throat.

"Sara is pregnant; Maya and I were planning her wedding and baby shower. You did not know that I am friends with Sara from high school Mr President."

"Whose precious baby is this then?" Dumbo was unconcerned.

"Aha guess wise men" Linda put her hands on her hips.

"I don't know much about that Sara woman, you tell me."

"It's Good old Caleb. Eat your heart out my boss."

"No...Oooh!!" Dumbo bellowed.

"Yes...sss!!" Linda retorted.

****

At United Corporations HQ in Alaska. Start and Finish looked startled hearing the update from their informer Gary in Kush.

"Sara is expecting Caleb's baby."

"No...Oooh!!" Finish shouted.

"Yes...sss!!" Gary retorted.

Kush Daily Newspaper
To the Living

Kush rising from far and wide to a wedding that never is,
They come from far and wide to a funeral that is.
They cry gallant sons of Kush that live no more.
Respect and awe is all they have and memories evermore.

Sons of Kush once emerged now forever taken.
They hope and pray that this vision stand,
Kush needs this flicker to light the hearts of man.
Light it was that God made: And said He, it was good.

Light brings knowledge, wisdom for mankind's good.
Light up Kush let your children see.
Two sons of the soil sparked a light in Kush.
Their candle blew away but a flicker lights.

Pass the torch to next generation do not tire.
Keep on people of the soil keep Kush burning bright,
Remove wet logs, blow the smoke away
Shine Kush brightly for the kids' sake.

Let not anyone dim the light lest we fall into darkness.
Kush light up, remove the debris, blow the dust.
Come on kids come on troopers, don't despair,
For the future awaits for more enlightened souls.
Yes, our Children's lives matter.

"Read all about it. Read all about it!!"
Shouted the skinny paper –boy.
   "The late President Daniel Simba's best-
seller, out today, read all about it, Read all about
it, get your copy today '**Kush Rising**' read all
about it!!!"

EPILOGUE

Deep down in the Congo jungles, in a thick, dense foliage, two men hung precariously. It was a labyrinth of trees, they were hurt and bleeding. Strange looking tribesmen with machetes were working in unison, chanting while cutting the overgrowth. From their village, they saw a strange big metallic bird dive and burst into thick smoke and fire. It took them a week to reach the area near the incident. The rain was unrelenting as it poured and made visibility difficult. The tribesmen can hear sounds of a man shouting from a nearby thicket.

"Caleb, are you okay? Oh, my word we are alive …Ouch, my leg hurts." Daniel could barely move as he was covered in dry blood, shrubs and thick cobwebs. With a broken leg, all he could do was groan.

"We have been given a second chance, we have been given another lease of life." Daniel cried.

"Daniel, Daniel where are we. We survived yes we are alive." Caleb looked deranged as he frantically battled with lizards that kept poking at his face.

It was the honey from a hive which was dripping down the twigs. They ate strange fruits from a shrub that entwined itself like a hammock. The rain was God sent. It gathered in leaves and cooled the air, giving sweet sips to the marooned men.

"I can hear people singing, hang in there Daniel, help is coming. Thank you, God, you spared us. This is divine providence for Kush. Indeed our future matters. Our children's lives matter."

A flurry of rain pattered against the leaves and they started singing.............

To God be the glory for the great things he has done,
Praise the Lord. Let the earth hear his voice.

ABOUT THE AUTHOR

Grace Tee is CEO & founder of
Mighty Pen Visions
It's foundations are
(Tools Of Mass Enlightenment)
(Children's Lives Matter)
3rd World children's Education initiative.
(Supporting children with fees and books.)
Authored Pursuit of the good life A Hearts &
Minds Saga, Koko's 24/7 Day & Night Angels
Fruits of the spirit, Diet Of the soul.
http://www.mightypenvisions.com